Designing Rubrics for Mathematics

dxww

Eileen Depka

SkyLight
Professional Development

Arlington Heights, Illinois

Designing Rubrics for Mathematics

Published by SkyLight Professional Development
2626 S. Clearbrook Dr., Arlington Heights, IL 60005
800-348-4474 or 847-290-6600
Fax 847-290-6609
info@skylightedu.com
http://www.skylightedu.com

President: Carol Luitjens
Executive Editor: Chris Jaeggi
Senior Acquisitions Editor: Jean Ward
Editor: Jodi Keller
Project Coordinator: Anne Kaske
Cover Designer and Illustrator: David Stockman
Book Designer: Bruce Leckie
Production Supervisor: Bob Crump

LCCCN 20-010867
ISBN 1-57517-380-8

2834-X
Item Number 2228
Z Y X W V U T S R Q P O N M L K J I H G F E D C B A
09 08 07 06 05 04 03 02 01   15 14 13 12 11 10 9 8 7 6 5 4 3 2

There are
one-story intellects,
two-story intellects, and
three-story intellects with skylights.

All fact collectors, who have no aim beyond their facts, are

one-story minds.

Two-story minds
compare, reason, generalize,
using the labors of the fact collectors
as well as their own.

Three-story minds
idealize, imagine, predict—their best illumination comes from above,

through the skylight.

—Oliver Wendell Holmes

Contents

Acknowledgments

I'd like to acknowledge several people who were instrumental in the development of this book. Without these individuals, progress would have been difficult, if not impossible.

Many thanks to Kay Burke, who is the real reason I wrote this book. Kay is an inspiration and motivational force for all educators, and I appreciate the time and support she provided me.

Thanks to the students who gladly completed the tasks found in this book. Their enthusiastic participation and feedback allowed me to create and modify tasks to better meet their needs and lead them to higher levels of achievement.

Thanks to my colleagues and fellow teachers for their role in my growth. Thanks to Rick Osterhaus who challenges me to grow, forces me to learn, and helps me stretch my limits into unfamiliar areas. Thanks to Bruce Connolly for his flexibility and support while allowing me to increase my opportunities to learn and extend my potential. And thanks to Terry Brecklin for the knowledge and enthusiasm she offers while pursuing her own quest to help students excel.

Thanks also to my family—my husband Jeff, and our children, Jessica, Jonathan, and Monica—for their patience and understanding. They accepted the time commitment needed to write this book and did not seem to mind when I appeared to be permanently attached to my laptop.

Finally, thanks to my mother, Barbara Zerwinski, who has always viewed education as a high priority. She has dedicated her life to learning and to helping others understand. She is an inspiration to me.

Introduction

The State of Mathematics

In 1992, the National Assessment of Educational Progress (NAEP) presented a devastating report to the nation. Over 250,000 fourth-, eighth- and twelfth-grade students in 10,000 schools nationwide were tested in mathematics proficiency. While the results showed that the students had made significant gains in mathematics proficiency since a study two years prior, only 25 percent or fewer students were deemed as being proficient in mathematics. One-third of the students tested did not even reach the lowest level of performance.

The NAEP published another report in 1996 finding that students at all grade levels showed an increase in scores on the 1996 test, which emphasized reasoning and communication within the mathematical standards identified as priorities by the National Council of Teachers of Mathematics (NCTM). The report indicated that 64 percent of fourth-grade students performed at or above the basic level, 62 percent of eighth-grade students achieved that same level, and 69 percent of the twelfth-grade test takers were able to score at or above the basic level.

Although this report seemed to contain better findings than the 1992 report, the results showed that over 30 percent of the students tested were not able to achieve even a basic level of performance, which means they were unable to achieve "partial mastery of prerequisite knowledge and skills that are fundamental for proficient work at each grade" (NAEP 1996, 8). These results show that educators need to find instructional methods that are catalysts for breakthrough performance and in-depth mathematical understanding for all students.

In today's classroom, mathematics teachers need to teach mathematics differently from the way they were taught mathematics. The world has changed in many ways in recent years. The use and availability of computers and computer technology has multiplied, the Internet has become a common research and communication tool, and videos and video games have become popularized. As a result, students have grown accustomed to various forms of brain stimulation and have come to welcome such forms of stimulation. Teachers lecturing while students take notes and complete routine problems from a textbook does not produce mathematics proficiency in all students. Students are not making the mathematical gains they deserve by working in isolation to complete worksheets or watching the teacher complete problems on the board; these practices do not reach all students (Black 1994). As stated by O'Brien, students need to be active thinkers and not simply memorize the thinking of others (1999). Mathematics needs to make sense to students, and the best way for this to occur is through hands-on learning. Practices must change and new strategies must be employed to help today's students to be successful in mathematics.

Many changes have occurred in the years following the 1996 NAEP study. Suggestions for new educational practices and techniques have flourished. Research shows that the classroom teacher and the strategies employed can and do impact the learner. New strategies (such as actively involving students through the use of performance tasks and problems that provide real-world applications) help students gain a deeper understanding of concepts involved and allow them to be better able to transfer that knowledge to new situations. Metacognitive strategies or reflective pieces written by students are strategies that assist students in developing a new level of understanding because students learn to evaluate their thinking and the processes they use to arrive at solutions. Assessment results can be used to positively drive instruction, and gains in student achievement can be made when students take an active role in the learning process. However, in order to help students be successful, teachers must be willing to adjust, adapt, try new things, and teach in ways that they probably were not taught. Teachers need to step outside of their comfort zones to seek practices that will impact their students.

For educators, increasing student achievement must be a primary goal. Creating a nation of thinkers and active problem solvers who can use their skills in ways that demonstrate true understanding is crucial for student success outside the classroom. Relating schoolwork and textbooks to real-world situations helps students see a purpose for their education. Active engagement in the learning process helps students make the mathematical connections necessary for increased learning and understanding. Rubrics are a necessary tool for promoting student achievement because they provide students with a clear road map that shows how to achieve success by allowing learners to assess their work against criteria for various levels of performance.

About This Book

This book offers methods, techniques, and tasks that can be used to engage learners in the hands-on learning of mathematics. This book establishes the importance of using standards and benchmarks as educational targets to help students understand expected outcomes, and it stresses the importance of rubric development and the assessment process. The performance tasks actively engage the learners while allowing them to have fun in the process.

Each chapter concentrates on a different aspect of rubrics and the assessment process. Strategies and suggestions are based on the research and opinions of top educators and organizations.

The first section of every chapter lays the foundation for suggested practices. The second section, called the Rubric/Mathematics Application, suggests a performance task that relates to the information covered in the first section. A complete explanation of the application is provided, as well as the resources (e.g., task explanations, suggested procedures, rubrics, graphic organizers, charts, and assessments) necessary to implement the task in a classroom. An overview page (see Figure Intro.1) is included in each of the rubric/mathematics applications. This page encapsulates all the important information needed to carry out the performance task. The steps to each task are accompanied by thumbnail versions of the figures that make up the data charts, reflection pages, assessments, and rubrics for the task.

All the performance tasks in this book are based on the National Council of Teachers of Mathematics *Principles and Standards for School Mathematics* (2000). Standards are the backbone of mathematics education and are currently the basis of almost all mathematics education programs in the United States. (More information regarding mathematics standards and their connection to rubrics is discussed in chapter 2.) The various principles and standards each application focuses on are listed in the overview page. The mathematical application in each chapter is designed to allow students to demonstrate their level of understanding of the mathematics standards embedded in the application. Each application states a problem or task, which is to be solved using mathematical skill, reasoning, and communication. The application also includes suggested procedures. These can be used to give direction for students who are not as familiar with performance tasks. (Performance tasks are opportunities for students to apply what they have learned in a real-life application.) For tasks with several steps or for more complex tasks, a task explanation and suggested procedures page is provided to be handed out to students. Each chapter offers Internet resource links that can be used to promote technology research in the classroom, and figures are included in each application that can be copied for classroom

■ RUBRIC/MATHEMATICS APPLICATIONS OVERVIEW ■
Page Explanation

STANDARDS   Each project is linked to the NCTM Standards.

MATHEMATICS CONCEPTS   The concepts related to the performance are listed.

GRADE LEVELS   Suggested grade levels are stated, although they can be extended in both directions.

RELATED CURRICULAR AREAS   Any curricular areas the project relates to in addition to mathematics are listed.

MATERIALS NEEDED   This section lists any necessary supplies. It also states if computers are needed.

TASK   The problem is a situation presented to students that sets the stage for a math connection related to the real world.

SUGGESTED STUDENT PROCEDURES   The procedures outline what students need to do to complete the task.

TEACHER RESOURCES   This is a list of the resource pages included in the chapter. The list indicates the pages that can be used with students.

INTERNET RESOURCES   Each Rubric/Mathematics Application includes several Web sites that are excellent resources for math teachers and students.

Figure Intro.1

use. Each application also contains information about how long it will generally take to complete. (Though provided as a number of 45-minute class periods, this time estimation may vary according to the level of the students, if calculators and/or computers are used, and depending on whether teachers incorporate the task extensions.)

All of the mathematics applications in this book have been used with students and have produced outstanding results. Students who need to be challenged have found that the applications allowed them to grow and extend their capabilities, and students who find mathematics difficult have successfully completed the applications and developed a deeper understanding of mathematical concepts and their use. Extensions and simplifications are provided so each application can be differentiated for individual classrooms, students, and grade levels. In this way, low achievers, as well as gifted students, are able to achieve beneficial results. Expansions are also offered that help extend the performance task into other curricular areas, such as language arts, art, and social studies. Such expansions are important as they incorporate an integrated, multiple intelligences (Gardner 1983) approach to learning. Technology is incorporated throughout the book in many uses; as a reference tool (to locate answers), as a construction tool (to build charts, graphs, or graphic organizers), and as a research tool (to find data).

Teachers can make a difference in the achievement level of their students by providing them with experiences that have an impact on their learning and performance. Students who become engaged in learning through active involvement develop an in-depth understanding of mathematics, how it relates to them, and how it influences the world. The strategies and applications provided throughout this book can help teachers assist students in this process.

Using Rubrics in Mathematics

The Rubric

According to *The New Merriam-Webster Dictionary* (Merriam-Webster 1989), a rubric is a heading, title, class, or category. In education, however, it means so much more. A rubric is a scoring guide that can be used to make reliable judgments about a student's product or performance. It is a tool that distinguishes the difference between teaching and learning by clearly stating criteria and describing levels of quality.

According to Schmoker (1996), rubrics allow individuals to assess and track numerical data in an expanded way. Schmoker explains that rubrics can assess thinking skills, student understanding, and students' ability to apply their knowledge to mathematical tasks. The rubric gives teachers, students, and parents a reliable picture of what students should know and be able to do as well as to what extent they are able to demonstrate their knowledge. Schmoker also states that a rubric—a set of written criteria used to analyze the outcomes of a student's learning—is "one of the most promising developments in assessment" (70). Rubrics are based on educational standards and expectations and address not only what a student is expected to know and be able to do, but also at what level of quality he or she is expected to perform.

Rubrics are built on a rating scale. Scales can vary, often ranging from 1 to 4, 0 to 3, or 1 to 6. The use of a specific scale is often a personal preference. The scale of 1–4 is probably the most common because it is small enough so students are not overwhelmed by descriptors, yet broad enough to encompass a wide range of quality descriptors. The scale of 0–3 is typically used when the rubric creator wants to use a zero to represent no progress being made by a student toward a specific criterion. Larger scales, such as 1–6, are used when products are more involved and there is opportunity for a more widespread level of performance.

Rating scales contain concise descriptions for each level of progress. These criteria, or performance indicators, clearly state the level of performance expected at each numerical value on the rubric. The criteria stated within the rubric can help the assessor accurately evaluate the student's work. Students too can use this tool to self-assess and improve their level of performance. The purpose of the rubric is not only to evaluate, but also to help students to grow and increase their level of performance by outlining a vision of success.

There are two types of rubrics: the analytic rubric and the holistic rubric. The analytic format uses multiple descriptors for each criterion evaluated within the rubric (see Figure 1.1). In essence, the student's product has multiple opportunities to be evaluated within the same rubric. In an analytic rubric, "a performance is assessed several times, using the lens of a separate criterion each time" (McTighe and Wiggins 1999, 273).

Example of Analytic Rubric

	0	**1**	**2**	**3**
Graph Title	Not titled	Partially or inaccurately titled	Titled with spelling or mechanical error	Titled accurately
Axes Title	Not titled	Titles present but inappropriate	Titles present with spelling or mechanical error	Titled accurately
X-axis Information	Not labeled or numbered	Labels or numbers present but inappropriate	Labels or numbers present with spelling or mechanical error	Labeled or numbered accurately
Y-axis Information	Not labeled or numbered	Labels or numbers present but inappropriate	Labels or numbers present with spelling or mechanical error	Labeled or numbered accurately
Key	Not present	Present but incomplete	Present with inaccuracies	Present and accurate
Graphed According to Key	No correspondence to key	Much graphed inaccurately	Graphed with minor error	Graphed according to key
Accuracy of Graph	Graph incomplete	Graph complete with several errors	Graph complete with 1–2 errors	Graph complete and accurate

Figure 1.1

A holistic rubric (see Figure 1.2) has one performance expectation description at each numerical level on the rubric. The product or performance is evaluated as a whole and often given a single score. The holistic rubric is, then, "a rubric used to obtain the overall impression of the quality of a performance or product" (McTighe and Wiggins 1999, 277).

Analytic rubrics are best used as a part of the formative process. These rubrics are specifically designed as tools to improve student achievement through their use during any task or performance. Students are able to rely on the rubric descriptors to increase their level of performance. Holistic rubrics, in turn, are summative in nature. This type of rubric is most often used to evaluate work only at the end of a process. All rubrics used within this book are analytic rubrics, as these are the types of rubrics that best help to increase student performance.

Example of Holistic Rubric

ORAL PRESENTATION RUBRIC

Name:_____   Date:_____

Subject:_____   Final Grade:_____

5
The subject is addressed clearly
Speech is loud enough and easy to understand
Good eye contact
Visual aid is used effectively
Well-organized

4
Subject is addressed adequately
Speech has appropriate volume
Eye contact is intermittent
Visual aid helps presentations
Good organization

3
Subject is addressed adequately
Speech volume is erratic
Student reads notes—erratic eye contact
Visual aid does not enhance speech
Speech gets "off track" in places

2
Speech needs more explanation
Speech is difficult to understand at times
Lack of adequate eye contact
Poor visual aid
Lack of organization

1
Speech does not address topic
Speech cannot be heard
Very little eye contact
No visual aid
No organization

Scale: 5 = A; 4 = B; 3 = C; 2 = D; 1 = Not Yet
General Comments:

Adapted from *The Mindful School: How to Assess Authentic Learning* by Kay Burke © 1999 IRI/SkyLight Training and Publishing, Inc. Reprinted by permission of SkyLight Professional Development, Arlington Heights, IL.

Figure 1.2

Why Use Rubrics in Mathematics?

A myth surrounds the teaching of mathematics that is thought to be true by all too many. This myth is that if the curriculum is covered, students will learn. Of course, all good mathematics teachers realize this is not the case, but often it is difficult for teachers to know what to do to better help students internalize the material. Teachers often wonder how students make mathematics their own and how they can help students personalize and make sense of mathematical concepts.

Student learning and understanding is often directly related to the variety of experiences within the mathematics classroom. According to Battista (1999), traditional methods in teaching mathematics fail to help students make connections to other situations where a mathematical formula might apply. Traditional methods have also proven to be ineffective as shown by the National Assessment of Educational Progress (NAEP) test results (see the Introduction). Students must be given numerous opportunities to form solid mathematical connections by solving real-world problems and making real-life applications.

In the traditional mathematics classroom, student work solely involved doing calculations. Answers were right or wrong, and as a result, grading was fairly simplistic. These techniques, however, are not fulfilling students' mathematical needs. National studies have shown that students from the United States are not competitive in mathematics worldwide. Studies such as those done by the NAEP have shown that a high percentage of students are unable to understand mathematics at a basic level. Adults in the US often admit that they do not understand, and never will understand, mathematics. These indicators demonstrate that traditional mathematics methods may have done a good job of teaching calculations, but a poor job of teaching thinking and application. Therefore, the focus in mathematics today has become one of active involvement, where students are not only able to calculate, but also to think, apply, and explain their actions and processes.

According to Bryant and Driscoll (1998), "Open-ended questions and other alternative assessments go further, which allows for richer responses from students and better data about students' mathematical content knowledge and problem solving skills. This information helps to inform teachers about where students are and what instruction they need to concentrate on. In order to be useful for the teacher, those data must be skillfully interpreted" (27). Rubrics are the necessary tool for this type of skillful interpretation. Rubrics assess student outcomes and encourage student growth, enhanced performance, and increased levels of understanding. Through the use of clear, precise descriptors, student output can be categorized according to level of performance or understanding and a point value can be assigned to that level. Students can use rubrics prior to project completion to identify levels of quality and can use rubric descriptors to enhance their performance.

Increased use of a variety of performance tasks and analytic rubrics can be the key to increased student understanding and achievement, because rubrics give students prior notice of the expectations for a given task or performance. Teachers should keep in mind that they need to share rubrics with students in advance of a task. Discussing the criteria with students is important so rubrics do not become a top-down system like most assessments. If the indicators of success are not shared before the assignment begins, the rubric loses its effectiveness in aiding student success. Rubrics encourage quality by giving students access to clearly defined criteria and levels of performance. Rubrics also make students aware of the effort and accomplishment required to complete a task successfully. Through the use of various tasks and performances, students internalize mathematical concepts because they are engaging in the process of learning instead of simply memorizing the process used to reach an answer. They see the relationship between a concept and its real-world applications and demonstrate a level of understanding far beyond a page of calculations.

Regarding the benefits of using rubrics, Schmoker (1996) states that by clearly defining a performance, students see it as achievable. The rubric also provides students and parents with feedback that clearly identifies strengths and weaknesses—a characteristic that is not a strong point of traditional grading practices.

Rubrics help promote the goal of a sound education in mathematics, which includes developing "powerful mathematical thinking in students, [and] instruction [that] must focus on, guide, and support their personal construction of ideas. Such instruction encourages students to invent, test, and refine their own ideas" (Battista 1999, 430). Rubrics are the evaluation tool necessary to aid in this task, because they provide students with a guide to success and encourage them to reach for their goals.

The performances and tasks that encourage student success are found throughout this book as Rubric/Mathematics Applications. Each Mathematics Application section outlines a mathematical task that puts rubrics into practice. The application for this chapter is entitled You're Right On Target!

— ∞ —

RUBRIC/MATHEMATICS APPLICATION

You're Right on Target!

You're Right on Target! is a task created to enhance skills in coordinate graphing. The application is based on three mathematics standards: geometry and spatial sense, communication, and problem solving. These standards, which are highlighted on the overview page, are addressed during completion of the task.

This rubric/mathematics application is written at three levels of difficulty: primary, middle, and high school. Each figure provided is adapted to meet these three different levels. These levels can also be used as a way to differentiate within a multilevel or multiability classroom. Students who need to be challenged can work at level three, students who are capable can work at level two, and students who need more foundational skills might function best at level one.

The application creates a problem for students to solve that requires the use of a variety of mathematical and communication skills. It may be presented to students with or without the suggested procedures listed within the overview. Students who are inexperienced in dealing with performance tasks or those who require more guidance will benefit from knowledge of the procedures. In classrooms where problem-based learning is commonplace, the task alone can be supplied.

For the best results with mathematics applications, review all written information, teaching tools, and resources prior to presenting the task to students. Flexibility and creativity are encouraged, and throughout the unit suggestions are made to assist in restructuring this task to fit the needs of individual classroom populations and teachers.

The teacher resources within this chapter include instructions for the students and explanations for the teacher. All mathematics applications have answer keys. If teachers need additional resources or more information about coordinate graphing, the Internet is an excellent tool. A few Web sites are listed within the overview (see Figure 1.3) to get teachers started.

PERFORMANCE TASK EXPLANATION

Students need to understand the meaning of coordinates and coordinate graphing before completing this task. During the completion of the task, students demonstrate an awareness and knowledge of graph numbering. During the task they locate the x- and y-axis and place stickers at the intersections of lines on the graph paper. Then, they accurately identify the coordinates at which the stickers are placed. This task takes about two to four fifty-five minute class periods depending on the use of expansion activities.

▪ UNIT OVERVIEW ▪
You're Right on Target!

STANDARDS Geometry and spatial sense, Communication, Problem Solving

MATHEMATICS CONCEPTS Coordinate graphing

GRADE LEVELS 2 through 10

RELATED CURRICULAR AREAS Social Studies—Map skills; Language Arts—Writing directions; Art—Design packaging

MATERIALS NEEDED Assorted stickers; grid paper (blackline master included)

TASK Quadrant Brothers Toy Company is in the process of creating a new strategy game. The game consists of locating hidden targets on a graph by guessing the location's coordinates. Players are given hints relating to the direction of the hidden targets. The game contains hundreds of different graphs. The company needs your help to create the graphs and target locations as well as to provide answer keys for the players.

SUGGESTED STUDENT PROCEDURES

1. Choose stickers and place them at line intersections at various locations on a piece of grid (graph) paper.
2. Label and number the x-axis (horizontal axis).
3. Label and number the y-axis (vertical axis).
4. Create a title for the graph.
5. Create an answer key for your graph that lists the coordinates where the stickers were placed. Place the coordinates on the chart provided.

TEACHER RESOURCES

Student task sheet for three levels
Student Answer Record Chart for three levels
Rubric for three levels
Graph checklist for all levels
Checkup and Key for three levels
Reflections for all levels

INTERNET RESOURCES

Math Matters: Contains information on combating mathematics anxiety, such as information on brain research and metalearning, as well as tips and strategies on helping students feel more comfortable with mathematics. <http://www.mathmatters.net/matips.htm>
Math Web Sites: Features links to over 100 mathematics Web sites. <http://www. spellman.com/edwebsites/Math.htm>
Quick Math Site (for higher levels): Provides help to mathematics questions in various areas, including graphing. <http://quickmath.com>

Figure 1.3

8

SkyLight Professional Development

The task is designed with three levels of difficulty. Younger students use large grid paper and twelve stickers. They use six stickers to identify coordinates and six stickers on their Student Record Charts. Students in the middle grades place twenty stickers on more detailed graph paper and list twenty coordinates. Students in the upper grades use four-quadrant graph paper and place thirty stickers on the paper, making certain that at least six stickers are placed in each quadrant. Students in every level identify the coordinates of all the stickers. The activity may be done as a class, in cooperative groups, or independently.

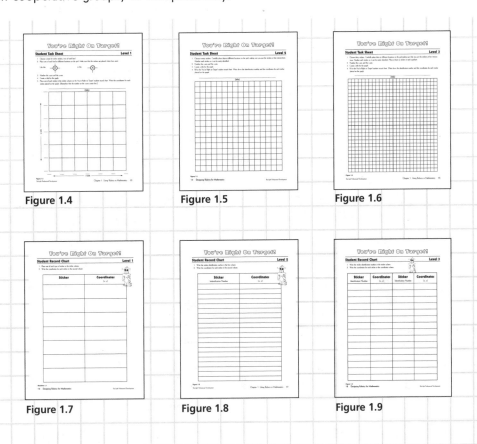

Figure 1.4   Figure 1.5   Figure 1.6

Figure 1.7   Figure 1.8   Figure 1.9

Figures 1.4–1.6 contain task sheets for all three levels, and Figures 1.7–1.9 contain the record charts for all three levels. In order to complete the activity, students should be given copies of the student task sheet and record chart. The record chart serves as a graphic organizer to help students organize their data and list coordinates. Students may want to create their own graphic organizer to house the information, and teachers should encourage this.

Teachers should make stickers available for the students. Large stickers may work better with younger students, while mini-stickers or dots may work better with older students who are using smaller-spaced graph paper. A time limit for choosing stickers can be given to students in advance to keep the task focused.

Figure 1.10

Figure 1.11

Figure 1.12

Figure 1.13

RUBRIC

Students should be aware of task expectations before beginning. Give each student or cooperative group a copy of the rubric, which is based on a 0 to 3 scale, from the start. Take a few minutes to highlight the expectations for the performance task. This will result in higher-quality products. The 3-point section on the rubric should be clear to the students so they understand how to aim for the highest level of achievement. Rubrics for each level are offered in Figures 1.10—1.12.

CHECKLIST

Students may begin the task after viewing the rubric. As students complete their graphs, the checklist (see Figure 1.13) of components to be demonstrated in the completed work provides reminders relating to all of the graph components.

Students should be given the opportunity to self-assess or peer assess before their work is turned in. The self-reflection prompted by rubric scoring results in students reaching for a higher level of quality. Students should be given a chance to enhance their performance by meeting high-level rubric descriptors. As students get used to using rubrics they become very good at peer evaluation and helping one another out. Sometimes students do not realize that they are missing a component and are very pleased when a peer points it out to them. This practice helps improve student performance and elevates students' level of achievement.

Peers and parents also can be encouraged to complete a rubric for task evaluation. Peer and parent reactions are especially beneficial when the rubric is used as a tool to assist students <u>before</u> the task is graded. Students can use parent and peer input to affirm, improve, and expand their product as necessary or appropriate.

Finally, the product should be submitted for teacher evaluation. When grading the finished products, teachers can circle or highlight the numerical rubric value most appropriate to the level of student performance. When rubrics are completed and a grade needs to be determined, the rubric score can be used as a grade or it can be converted into a percent by dividing the total points earned by the total points possible. The grading scale will vary depending on individual grading scales and scoring practices.

EXPANDING THE TASK

To extend this performance task into the area of language arts, ask students to write step-by-step directions for the game. Directions should include ways the game might best be organized and played. Emphasize creativity and clear communication skills. Students can also create game rules and strategies.

To extend this task into the art classroom, students can use their artistic skills to design packaging for the game, such as a game logo or a decorative cover. A large manila envelope can be used as a container for the game.

SIMPLIFYING THE TASK

The performance task is fairly simple and can be easily completed in one class period. However, if further simplification is needed, the task can be accomplished as a large or small group activity instead of independently. Another way to simplify is to ask students to identify fewer coordinates.

PLAYING THE GAME

Students can use their graphs to actually play the game. Each graph creator should be paired up with a classmate who guesses the coordinate location of a sticker. The graph creator tells the guesser if he or she is right or wrong. If the guesser is wrong, the creator gives the guesser a hint by telling him or her the direction to go in to get to the closest sticker. For example, the creator might tell the guesser that the closest sticker is to the southwest, or he or she might tell the guesser that the sticker is someplace west of three and north of five. Guessers should keep track of their guesses in order to make plans for future responses. Guessers need a blank piece of graph paper to do this.

The game can be played as an entire class with younger students. Using large graph paper, one side of the room can become the creators and the other side the guessers. Roles can be switched after the first game is complete.

CHECKUP

The checkup for each level is shown in Figures 1.14–1.16. These checkups are teacher-made assessments that can be used as practice tasks or tests. Students are asked to identify the coordinates of points on a grid. The task is designed at three

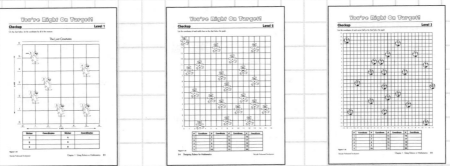

Figure 1.14   **Figure 1.15**   **Figure 1.16**

Figure 1.17

Figure 1.18

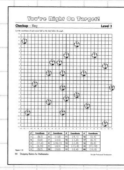

Figure 1.19

Figure 1.20

levels of difficulty. Using the task before the game shows if students have the skills necessary to complete the activity. Using it as a post-activity assessment determines if students understand coordinates and their relationship to a fixed position on a graph. Answer keys to the tests are provided in Figures 1.17–1.19.

MATHEMATICS REFLECTION

The mathematics reflection page (see Figure 1.20) can be used as a brief follow-up activity. The page asks students what they learned and what they liked about the task they have just completed. It is a form of metacognition, or thinking about thinking, and is similar to a journal entry.

Metacognition is a valuable tool because it helps students clearly articulate what they have learned as well as understand their strengths and weaknesses. Through the process of metacognition, students are challenged to understand their own thought processes and, as a result, are more likely to transfer their learning to other situations. A completed reflection page is provided in Figure 1.21 as an example of how students might reflect on this task.

Figure 1.21

— ∞ —

In Summary

The rubric is the tool that binds assessment and student achievement by making students and parents aware of expectations from the onset. When this occurs, achievement at a high level of performance is a natural outcome. There are no surprises for students during the evaluation process with the rubric.

Rubrics also make grading easier and less messy for teachers. Evaluation is not only about whether the answer is right or wrong, it is also about critiquing the steps used along the way. Rubrics provide teachers with clear guidelines to make the grading process less subjective and more concrete.

You're Right On Target!

Student Task Sheet
Level 1

1. Choose a total of twelve stickers, two of each kind.
2. Place one of each kind at different locations on the grid. Make sure that the stickers are placed where lines meet.

   Like this   or this

3. Number the x-axis and the y-axis.
4. Create a title for the graph.
5. Place one of each sticker in the sticker column on the Student Record Chart. Write the coordinates for each sticker placed on the graph. (Remember that the number on the x-axis comes first.)

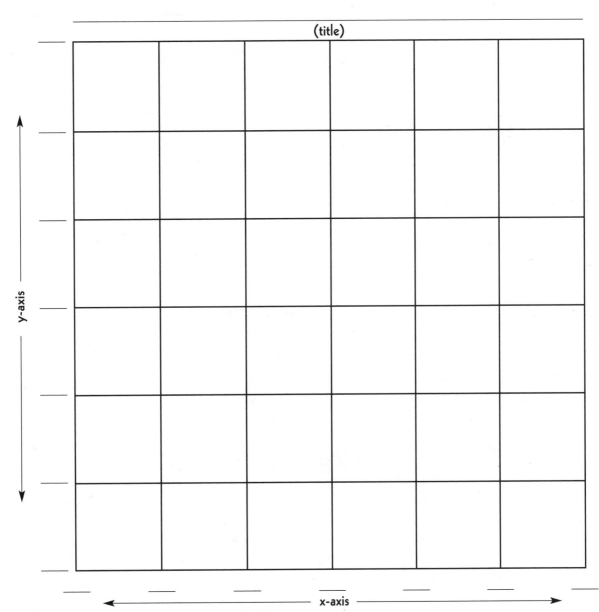

Figure 1.4

You're Right On Target!

1. Choose twenty stickers. Carefully place them at different locations on the grid, making sure you put the stickers at line intersections. Number each sticker so it can be easily identified.
2. Number the x-axis and the y-axis.
3. Create a title for the graph.
4. Fill in the Student Record Chart. Write down the identification number and the coordinates for each sticker placed on the graph.

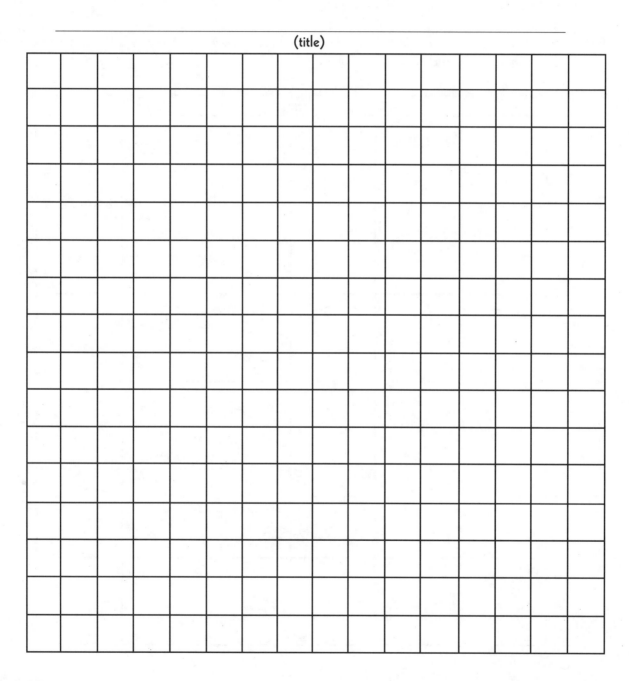

(title)

Figure 1.5

You're Right On Target!

1. Choose thirty stickers. Carefully place them at different locations on the grid making sure that you put the stickers at line intersections. Number each sticker so it can be easily identified. Place at least six stickers in each quadrant.

2. Number the x-axis and the y-axis.

3. Create a title for the graph.

4. Fill in the Student Record Chart. Write down the identification number and the coordinates for each sticker placed on the graph.

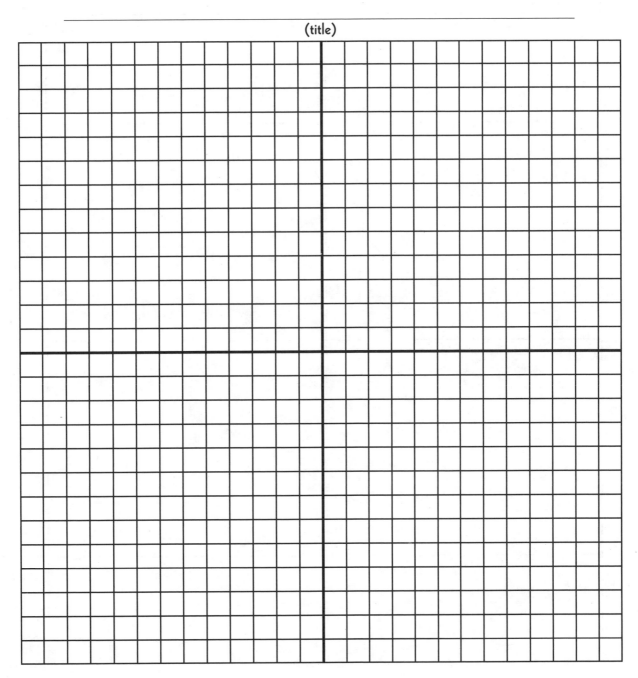

(title)

Figure 1.6

You're Right On Target!

1. Place one of each type of sticker in the sticker column.
2. Write the coordinates for each sticker in the second column.

Sticker	Coordinates (x, y)

Figure 1.7

You're Right On Target!

Student Record Chart — Level 2

1. Write the sticker identification number in the first column.
2. Write the coordinates for each sticker in the second column.

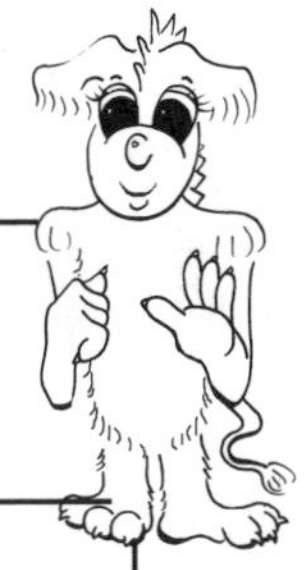

Sticker Indentification Number	**Coordinates** (x, y)

Figure 1.8

You're Right On Target!

1. Write the sticker identification number in the sticker column.
2. Write the coordinates for each sticker in the coordinates column.

Sticker Identification Number	**Coordinates** (x, y)	**Sticker** Identification Number	**Coordinates** (x, y)

Rubric

You're Right On Target!

Instructions: Choose the point value that best describes the performance in each category.

	0 You Missed!	1 You're on the edge!	2 You're getting closer!	3 You're right on target!	Points Earned
Graph Numbering x-axis	Not present or inaccurate	Complete	Complete, accurate	Complete, accurate, neat	_____
y-axis	Not present or inaccurate	Complete	Complete, accurate	Complete, accurate, neat	_____
Graph Title	Not present or inaccurate	Present with spelling and capitalization errors	Present with spelling or capitalization errors	Present with spelling and capitalization accurate	_____
Sticker Placement	Inaccurate placement of all stickers	1–2 stickers accurately placed on grid	3–5 stickers accurately placed on grid	All stickers accurately placed on grid	_____
Coordinates #1	Inaccurate	Accurate coordinates, missing comma and parentheses	Accurate coordinates, missing comma or parentheses	Accurate coordinates, including comma and parentheses	_____
#2	Inaccurate	Accurate coordinates, missing comma and parentheses	Accurate coordinates, missing comma or parentheses	Accurate coordinates, including comma and parentheses	_____
#3	Inaccurate	Accurate coordinates, missing comma and parentheses	Accurate coordinates, missing comma or parentheses	Accurate coordinates, including comma and parentheses	_____
#4	Inaccurate	Accurate coordinates, missing comma and parentheses	Accurate coordinates, missing comma or parentheses	Accurate coordinates, including comma and parentheses	_____
#5	Inaccurate	Accurate coordinates, missing comma and parentheses	Accurate coordinates, missing comma or parentheses	Accurate coordinates, including comma and parentheses	_____
#6	Inaccurate	Accurate coordinates, missing comma and parentheses	Accurate coordinates, missing comma or parentheses	Accurate coordinates, including comma and parentheses	_____

Points possible = 30   Points earned = _____

Evaluator: _____

Figure 1.10

Rubric

Instructions: Choose the point value that best describes the performance in each category.

	0 You Missed!	1 You're on the edge!	2 You're getting closer!	3 You're right on target!	Points Earned
Graph Numbering x-axis	Not present or inaccurate	Complete	Complete, accurate	Complete, accurate, neat	_____
y-axis	Not present or inaccurate	Complete	Complete, accurate	Complete, accurate, neat	_____
Graph Title	Not present or inaccurate	Present with spelling and capitalization errors	Present with spelling or capitalization errors	Present with spelling and capitalization accurate	_____
Sticker Placement	Inaccurate placement of all stickers	1–2 stickers accurately placed on grid	3–5 stickers accurately placed on grid	All stickers accurately placed on grid	
Coordinates #1–4	Inaccurate	1 accurate pair of coordinates, including comma and parentheses	2–3 accurate pairs of coordinates including comma and parentheses	All accurate coordinates, including comma and parentheses	_____
#5–8	Inaccurate	1 accurate pair of coordinates, including comma and parentheses	2–3 accurate pairs of coordinates including comma and parentheses	All accurate coordinates, including comma and parentheses	_____
#9–12	Inaccurate	1 accurate pair of coordinates, including comma and parentheses	2–3 accurate pairs of coordinates including comma and parentheses	All accurate coordinates, including comma and parentheses	_____
#13–16	Inaccurate	1 accurate pair of coordinates, including comma and parentheses	2–3 accurate pairs of coordinates including comma and parentheses	All accurate coordinates, including comma and parentheses	_____
#17–20	Inaccurate	1 accurate pair of coordinates, including comma and parentheses	2–3 accurate pairs of coordinates including comma and parentheses	All accurate coordinates, including comma and parentheses	_____
Neatness	Sloppy, difficult to read	Can be read with careful concentration	Neat, some room for improvement	Perfectly neat!	_____

Points possible = 30   Points earned = _____

Evaluator: _____

Figure 1.11

You're Right On Target!

Rubric

Level 3

Instructions: Choose the point value that best describes the performance in each category.

	0 You Missed!	1 You're on the edge!	2 You're getting closer!	3 You're right on target!	Points Earned
Graph Numbering x-axis	Not present or inaccurate	Complete	Complete, accurate	Complete, accurate, neat	_____
y-axis	Not present or inaccurate	Complete	Complete, accurate	Complete, accurate, neat	_____
Graph Title	Not present or inaccurate	Present with spelling and capitalization errors	Present with spelling or capitalization errors	Present with spelling and capitalization accurate	_____
Sticker Placement	Inaccurate placement of all stickers	1–2 stickers accurately placed on grid	3–5 stickers accurately placed on grid	All stickers accurately placed on grid	
Coordinates #1–6	Inaccurate	1 accurate pair of coordinates, including comma and parentheses	2–3 accurate pairs of coordinates including comma and parentheses	All accurate coordinates, including comma and parentheses	_____
#7–12	Inaccurate	1 accurate pair of coordinates, including comma and parentheses	2–3 accurate pairs of coordinates including comma and parentheses	All accurate coordinates, including comma and parentheses	_____
#12–18	Inaccurate	1 accurate pair of coordinates, including comma and parentheses	2–3 accurate pairs of coordinates including comma and parentheses	All accurate coordinates, including comma and parentheses	_____
#19–24	Inaccurate	1 accurate pair of coordinates, including comma and parentheses	2–3 accurate pairs of coordinates including comma and parentheses	All accurate coordinates, including comma and parentheses	_____
#25–30	Inaccurate	1 accurate pair of coordinates, including comma and parentheses	2–3 accurate pairs of coordinates including comma and parentheses	All accurate coordinates, including comma and parentheses	_____
Neatness	Sloppy, difficult to read	Can be read with careful concentration	Neat, some room for improvement	Perfectly neat!	_____

Points possible = 30   Points earned = _____

Evaluator: _____

Figure 1.12

You're Right On Target!

Graph Checklist

All Levels

Place an 'x' in the box that best describes the work you have completed on your graph.

	Yes!	I'm still working on it.
Graph has a title		
Title is capitalized appropriately		
Title relates to graph		
x-axis is numbered		
Numbers are neat		
y-axis is numbered		
Numbers are neat		
All stickers are placed at various line intersections		
All coordinates are complete		
x-axis number is the first coordinate		
Coordinates are in parentheses		
A comma is between coordinates		

Is your work complete? Check the checklist.

Figure 1.13

You're Right On Target!

On the chart below, list the coordinates for all of the creatures.

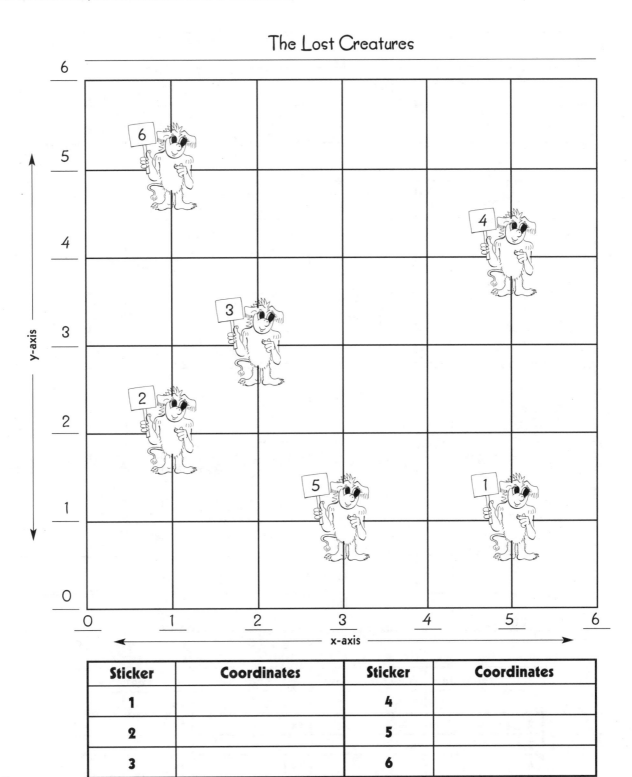

Sticker	Coordinates	Sticker	Coordinates
1		4	
2		5	
3		6	

Figure 1.14

You're Right On Target!

List the coordinates of each teddy bear on the chart below the graph.

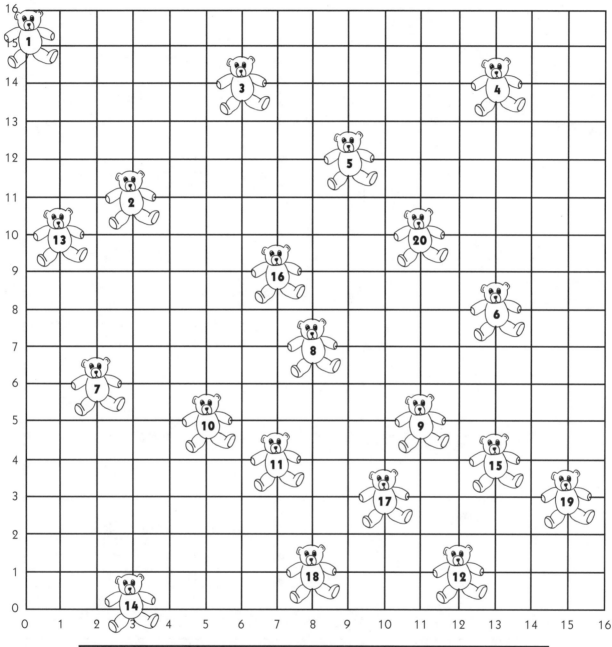

#	Coordinate	#	Coordinate	#	Coordinate	#	Coordinate
1		6		11		16	
2		7		12		17	
3		8		13		18	
4		9		14		19	
5		10		15		20	

Figure 1.15

You're Right On Target!

List the coordinates of each soccer ball on the chart below the graph.

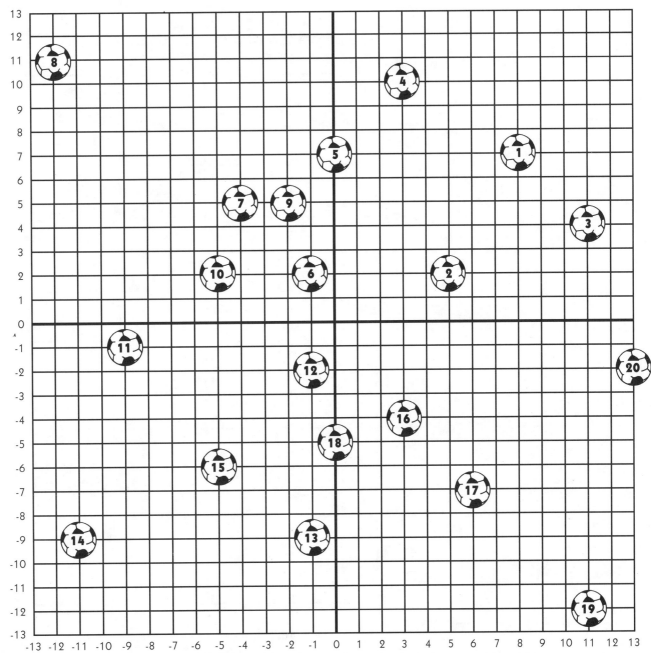

#	Coordinate	#	Coordinate	#	Coordinate	#	Coordinate
1		6		11		16	
2		7		12		17	
3		8		13		18	
4		9		14		19	
5		10		15		20	

Figure 1.16

You're Right On Target!

On the chart below, list the coordinates for all of the creatures.

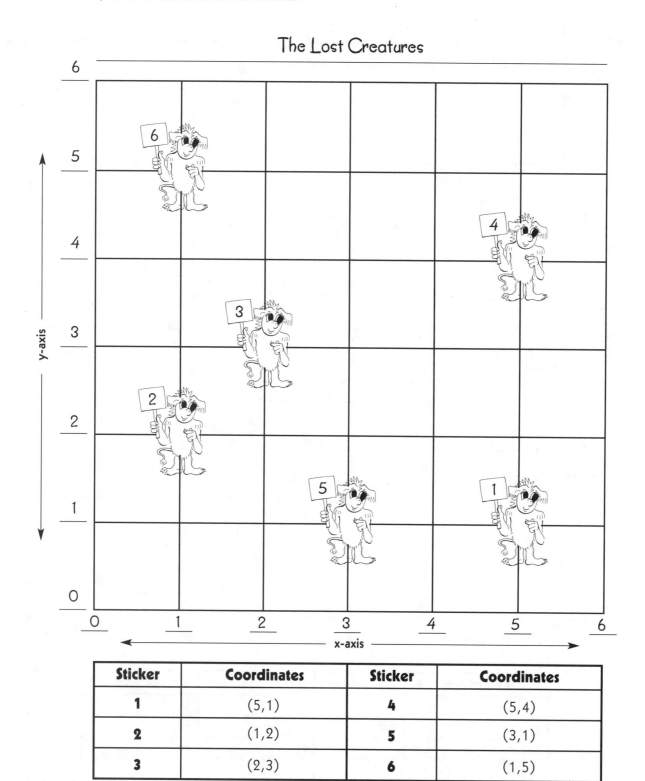

The Lost Creatures

Sticker	Coordinates	Sticker	Coordinates
1	(5,1)	**4**	(5,4)
2	(1,2)	**5**	(3,1)
3	(2,3)	**6**	(1,5)

Figure 1.17

You're Right On Target!

List the coordinates of each teddy bear on the chart below the graph.

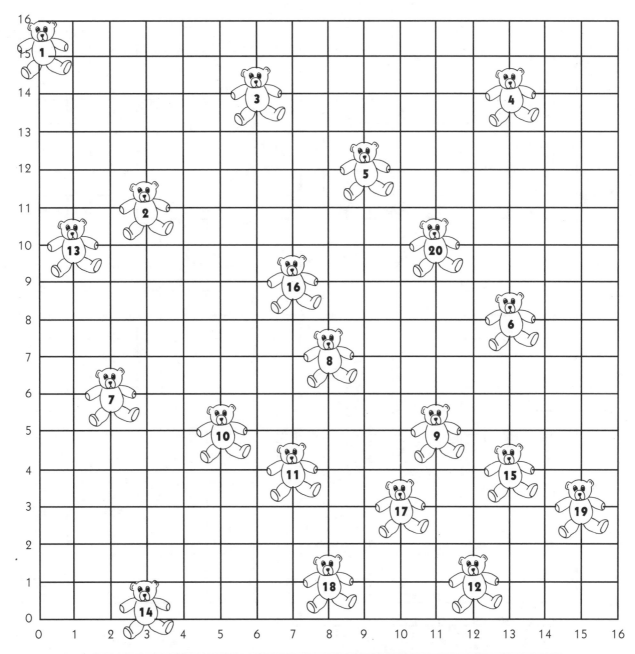

#	Coordinate	#	Coordinate	#	Coordinate	#	Coordinate
1	(0,15)	6	(13,8)	11	(7,4)	16	(7,9)
2	(3,11)	7	(2,6)	12	(12,1)	17	(10,3)
3	(6,14)	8	(8,7)	13	(1,10)	18	(8,1)
4	(13,14)	9	(11,5)	14	(3,0)	19	(15,3)
5	(9,12)	10	(5,5)	15	(13,4)	20	(11,10)

Figure 1.18

You're Right On Target!

List the coordinates of each soccer ball on the chart below the graph.

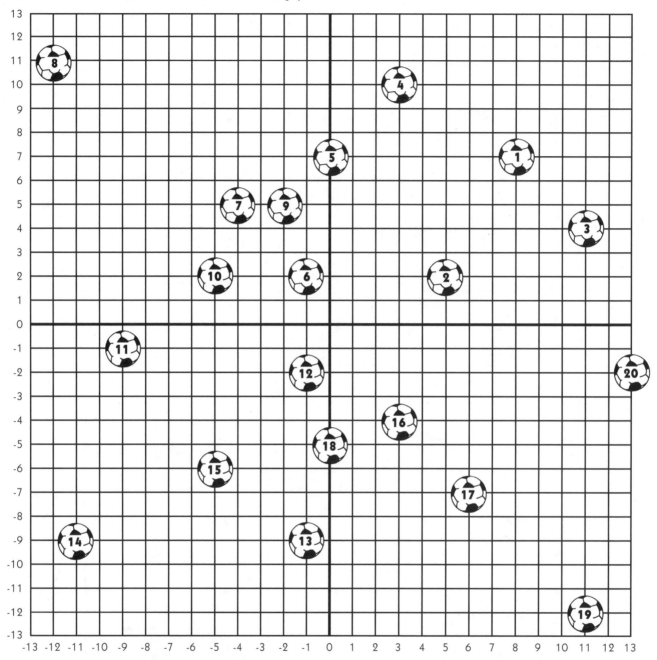

#	Coordinate	#	Coordinate	#	Coordinate	#	Coordinate
1	(8,7)	6	(-1,2)	11	(-9,-1)	16	(3,-4)
2	(5,2)	7	(-4,5)	12	(-1,-2)	17	(6,-7)
3	(11,4)	8	(-12,11)	13	(-1,-9)	18	(0,-5)
4	(3,10)	9	(-2,5)	14	(-11,-9)	19	(11,-12)
5	(0,7)	10	(-5,2)	15	(-5,-6)	20	(13,-2)

Figure 1.19

You're Right On Target!

Reflections

All Levels

In the space provided write your reflections on the graphing task.

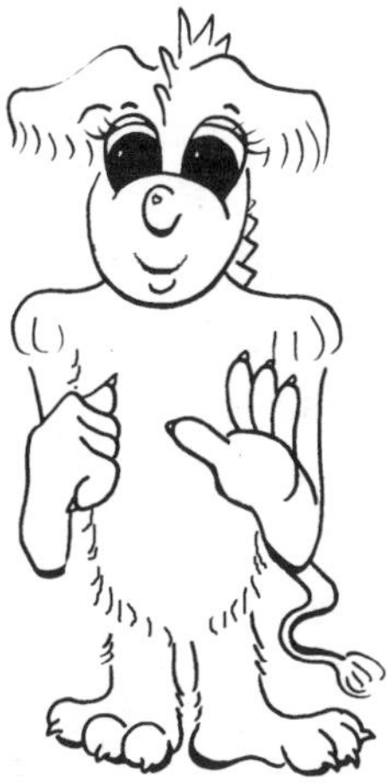

I learned: ____

____

____

____

____

____

____

____

____

I liked: ____

____

____

____

____

____

____

____

____

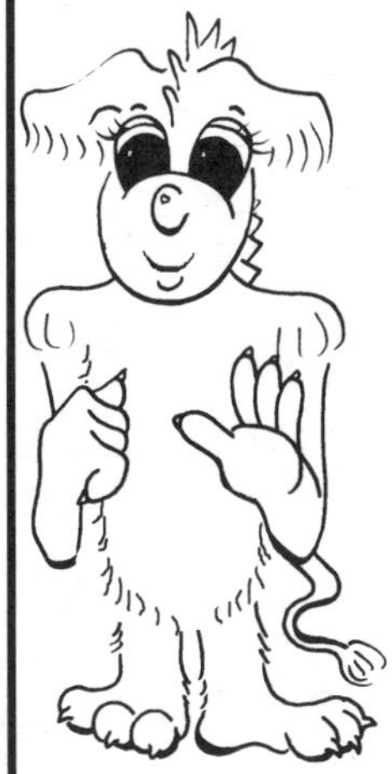

Figure 1.20

You're Right On Target!

In the space provided write your reflections on the graphing task.

I learned: _____

　　　　Lots of things about coordinate graphing
and labeling graphs. I know how to place points
without mistakes.

_____

_____

_____

_____

_____

I liked: _____

　　　　The game. It was fun to have someone guess where
my stickers were. I had fun guessing, too. I can remember
coordinates better now. I know the x comes before the
y and x is on the horizontal axis.

_____

_____

_____

Figure 1.21

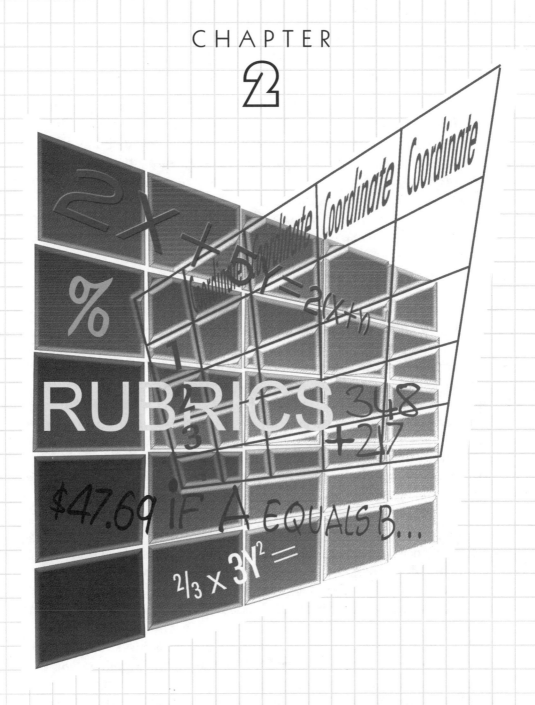

The Relationship Between Mathematics Standards and Rubrics

The Importance of Standards

When a house is built, a strong foundation is of utmost importance. Without it, the structure is unstable, unpredictable, and perhaps even unsafe. In education, standards form the foundational framework. They keep the structure solid and dependable. Standards guarantee students that their education is built on firm ground and is consistent with the education being received by others.

Standards are the educational guidelines for instruction and provide educators with the broad expectations students should achieve. Standards are broad categories of knowledge that experts deem essential to learning in specific fields of study. In the *Principles and Standards for School Mathematics* (2000), the National Council of Teachers of Mathematics (NCTM) identified ten standards—five content and five process. The five content standards include numbers and operations, algebra, geometry, measurement, and data analysis and probability. The process standards include problem solving, reasoning and proof, communication, connections, and representation. Identifying and using standards is crucial to teaching mathematics throughout the United States because standards provide a mathematical focus for instruction. Ideally, with the widespread use of standards, all students throughout the country are guaranteed the same mathematical concept focus. Currently, forty-nine states have adopted standards for their educational systems.

According to Fitzpatrick (1998), a coherent vision of student learning is necessary in order for a program of study to maintain focus. With standards as the focus, the foundation needed to create learning experiences that promote excellence in education and impact student performance is in place.

Benchmarks go hand in hand with standards. Benchmarks are more specific and indicate performance expectations for every student. Benchmarks are expectations that describe what students should know and be able to do within each standard. For example, according to the NCTM (2000), a geometry standard at the third- and fifth-grade level states that students should "apply transformations and use symmetry to analyze mathematical situations" (164). A more specific expectation or benchmark indicates that students should "predict and describe the results of sliding, flipping, and turning two-dimensional shapes" (164).

Together, standards and benchmarks are the vision of lesson outcomes. They let educators know in advance the essential knowledge required for a lesson to be considered successful. Standards and benchmarks help increase student performances, because they indicate the expectations for all students. Student performance and achievement is compared to standards and benchmarks, and that comparison can then be used as a measurement of success. With standards and benchmarks, high expectations are present for all students and all are expected to achieve. When there is a genuine commitment to standards-based achievement, comparing students to the average becomes truly unnecessary (Reeves 1998). Students in a standards-based classroom are not compared to other students to determine their standing in the class or their grade on a performance because the standards provide the basis for comparison.

The goal of standards-based education is for all students to be winners and perform to their highest potential. All students are aware of the standards they need to reach; the educator's job is to assist them on their road to achievement. State and district standards and benchmarks clearly define expectations; educators provide experiences that assist students in understanding concepts and constructing meaning according to the expectations outlined within the standards and benchmarks (Zemelman, Daniels, and Hyde 1993). Teachers can provide such experiences by using performance tasks and providing real-life experiences for their students. These types of tasks are discussed further in chapter 3.

Mathematics Standards and Rubrics

According to the NCTM, standards are a prototype that can be viewed as a professional consensus of what is deemed important to the understanding of mathematics (Crosswhite et al. 1989). The standards are a compilation of what educators have endorsed as the practices and concepts necessary to create a sound mathematics program. The NCTM standards provide guidance for daily classroom experiences, and most schools use standards that are based on those compiled by the NCTM. The NCTM document *Principles and Standards for School Mathematics* (2000) contains five standards that reflect crucial mathematical content, and an additional five process standards that emphasize mathematical learning and understanding. Process standards aim to ensure that students can go beyond computation into mathematical interpretation, problem solving, and communication to develop a deep understanding of mathematical concepts. The NCTM standards are used as the basis for all mathematics units within this book, and they are also the mathematics standards used by educational systems throughout the United States. While schools or districts may present their mathematics standards in a different format from the NCTM standards, the concepts are the same as those found in the NCTM. For more information on the NCTM standards, go to <www.nctm.org>.

Using the district or state standards and benchmarks for the grade level as a guide, teachers must determine the specific skills and essential knowledge to be learned prior to developing an instructional plan. Doing this helps to successfully develop a quality task. Teachers can use the rubric as an organizational tool to display criteria and show explicit expectations for a quality performance. The rubric allows teachers to organize the benchmarks into a format that students can use as guidelines in a learning application. While standards establish the focus of the learning, the rubric provides the evaluation tool.

Creating a Rubric that Addresses Standards

When developing a rubric, it is important for teachers to keep in mind a picture of exemplary student performance. Teachers can consider questions such as:

- What will success look like?
- What are the expected levels of quality?
- How will students transition from practice and memorization to reasoning?

The rubric should contain clearly stated descriptions of mastery. The rubric should also discriminate between each level of performance (Bryant and Driscoll 1998). The majority of performance tasks address several standards, and within those standards one or more benchmarks apply. The criteria should relate to these benchmarks.

When designing a rubric, teachers should list all criteria that are important to the task and include all the concepts and accomplishments crucial to successfully completing the performance. It is imperative that the criteria are tied directly to the standards and benchmarks. For example, a geometry standard states that students should "specify locations and describe spatial relationships using coordinate geometry and other representational systems" and the benchmark is that students can "make and use coordinate systems to specify locations and to describe paths" (NCTM 2000, 164). The criteria in the rubric should include specifics that provide evidence that students are able to demonstrate understanding of the benchmark. In the case of making a coordinate graph, such a list might include criteria important to the understanding of a graph: a title, axes titled, x- and y-axes numbered accurately, a key (if necessary), and coordinates graphed accurately. Achieving the targeted criteria is the prevailing goal of any task.

The next step is to set the ideal—determine the highest level of quality. The questions to consider when doing this include:

- What does the top level of achievement look like for each criterion?
- How can it be described?

This information should be entered in the greatest numerical level on the rubric. This level should become the expectation for all students.

In order to complete the creation of the rubric, teachers must make decisions regarding what other levels of performance look like as well. Each numerical level should contain a clearly stated description of performance, and each consecutive level should be a step closer to a quality product. In other words, each consecutive level should contain information to bring the product a step closer to the quality desired. The rubric should be a tool that guides its user to an exemplary end piece by defining the levels of expectation with quality descriptors. In order for the rubric to be an effective tool, it is imperative that the rubric be written in language that students can understand; it should be easy to use and clearly stated; and all levels of performance should build on each other so when a product is appraised, the evaluator is clear as to where it fits on the scale.

Before beginning a task, students should be taught how to use the rubric that will be used to evaluate the task. They need to clearly understand the expectations outlined for them. The best way for teachers to do this is to show examples of quality performances while pointing out the corresponding criteria on the rubric. This helps students visualize what a top-notch performance might look like. The rubric should be used throughout task completion to provide students with clearly articulated performance expectations and to help students maintain focus on the target.

The following rubric/mathematics application, How Negative Are Your Temperatures?, targets the standards of numbers and operation, measurement, communication and problem solving.

— ∞ —

RUBRIC/MATHEMATICS APPLICATION

How Negative are My Temperatures?

This rubric/mathematics application is most appropriate for students who are at an age level where integer operations are taught. Most likely this will be students in grades six through ten. Younger students who need a challenge or who are working at an advanced pace might also find that the application meets their needs. Further suggestions for simplification and extension can be found within the application explanations. An overview of the application is provided in Figure 2.1.

PERFORMANCE TASK EXPLANATION

In order to complete this application, students should be able to compare integers and add and subtract integers. During the task, students have ample opportunity to practice integer manipulations, demonstrate their own capabilities, and explain the procedures they used when working with integers. This performance task takes about two to three 45-minute class periods.

To begin the performance task, students need to locate and collect the data necessary to complete the task. Because the object of the assignment is to work with integers, students need to search for information about a state that experiences subzero winter temperatures. The data collection process might begin with an Internet search of weather information to locate an appropriate site. This could be done using the keyword <u>weather</u>. Students can also e-mail local weather personalities and ask for sites that contain the data required. (If teachers choose to have students do this, they should have students send their e-mail several days before starting the task so that e-mail recipients have time to respond.)

Figure 2.2

Another option is for students to use the Web site listed in the suggested student procedures in the overview. When doing their research, students search for the daily record high and low temperatures for the month of January. Student findings can be recorded on the organizational chart provided in Figure 2.2, or students may wish to create their own graphic organizer.

After recording data on the chart, students can begin their calculations. The difference between the record high temperature and the record low temperature should be determined for each day of the month. The temperatures should also be compared to find the lowest and highest temperature of the month. Students can show their calculations on a separate piece of paper.

36

▪ UNIT OVERVIEW ▪
How Negative Are My Temperatures?

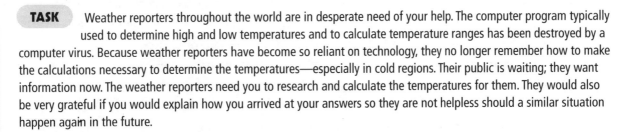

STANDARDS Numbers and Operations, Measurement, Communication, Problem Solving

MATHEMATICS CONCEPTS Compare integers, add and subtract integers

GRADE LEVELS 6 through 10

RELATED CURRICULAR AREAS Technology—Using the Internet; Language Arts—Writing an explanation

MATERIALS NEEDED Computer with Internet access

TASK Weather reporters throughout the world are in desperate need of your help. The computer program typically used to determine high and low temperatures and to calculate temperature ranges has been destroyed by a computer virus. Because weather reporters have become so reliant on technology, they no longer remember how to make the calculations necessary to determine the temperatures—especially in cold regions. Their public is waiting; they want information now. The weather reporters need you to research and calculate the temperatures for them. They would also be very grateful if you would explain how you arrived at your answers so they are not helpless should a similar situation happen again in the future.

SUGGESTED STUDENT PROCEDURES

1. Using the Internet, find the record high and low temperatures for January in Wisconsin or another state with extreme winter temperatures. (One possible Web site is <www.crh.noaa.gov>.)
2. Identify the warmest and the coldest temperature for the month.
3. Find the differences between the record high and record low temperatures for each day of the month.
4. Clearly explain the procedures used for adding and subtracting integers. Give examples. Include an explanation of the method used to compare integers in order to identify the high and low temperatures for the month.
5. Organize all information on a poster or visual display. You may want to include a calendar, easy-to-understand charts, or graphic organizers (a graphic display of your findings).

TEACHER RESOURCES

High and Low Temperature Record Organizer
Adding and Subtracting Integers Student Helpers #1 and #2
Rubric

Checkups 1 and 2 and Answer Keys
Integer Challenge and Key

INTERNET RESOURCES

Discovery School: Offers homework helpers for students and creative mathematics curriculum resources for teachers. <http://www.school.discovery.com>

Lycos Zone: Offers an interactive mathematics test students can take online for addition, subtraction, multiplication, or division. <http://bonus.lycos.com/bonus/card/Math_Test_game.html>

Math Goodies: Provides interactive mathematics lessons, homework helpers, puzzles, worksheets and more. <http://www.mathgoodies.com>

Figure 2.1

Figure 2.3

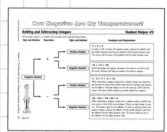

Figure 2.4

Figure 2.5

After completing all calculations, students need to explain the procedures used to compare the integers and the methods used to add and subtract integers. Explanations should be written and clear examples should be provided. Students should create their own organizational tool to record this information. Two graphic organizers (Figures 2.3 and 2.4) highlighting the procedures used when adding and subtracting integers are included in this chapter and can be used as teaching tools or examples. These student samples might be best used before beginning the task as a way to help students remember the processes for adding and subtracting integers.

RUBRIC

Students should always be aware of the characteristics of success when beginning an application. In order to meet and exceed the expectations for the task, students need to be aware of all aspects of the performance, including the grading piece. Every student or cooperative group of students needs to have a copy of the rubric from the start. This rubric (see Figure 2.5) is based on a 0 to 3 scale. Taking a few minutes of class time to read through the descriptors on the rubric results in higher-quality products. Make the 3-point section on the rubric clear to the students so they aim for the highest level of achievement. Give students time to ask questions.

When grading the finished products, simply circle or highlight the numerical value that is the most accurate description of the performance. The individual criteria scores should be added to determine the final score achieved on the rubric.

EXPANDING THE TASK

To expand the performance task, ask students to find average temperatures for each week of the month. This requires knowledge of the operations of multiplication and division of decimals. Information should be organized and recorded by the students. Students should also be prepared to explain the methods used when multiplying and dividing integers.

Students might also research temperatures in another country and compare them to the temperatures used to complete the original performance task.

SIMPLIFYING THE TASK

To simplify the performance task, students could limit their research and calculations to the first week of the month. Identifying the high temperature and low temperature of one week might be a good task for younger students.

SHORTENING THE TASK

If time is limited, the students might work only on the mathematics aspect of the task. Depending on the age level of the students, completing the research and doing the mathematical calculations can be finished in one or two class periods. Students can eliminate the written explanation and the visual display, if necessary. This, however, is an important part of the task and helps determine if students fully grasp the concepts involved. The extra time is worth the depth of understanding students gain in the process. Explaining thinking is a metacognitive strategy that helps students clarify their thoughts and solidify their knowledge.

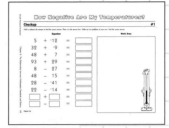

Figure 2.6

CHECKUP

The activities in Figures 2.6 and 2.7 can be used as an assignment or an assessment. If used before the performance task, the checkup can determine if the students are ready to complete the task. If used after the task as an assessment, the activity provides another indication of the students' ability to perform computations accurately when asked to add and subtract integers. Keys to these activities are offered in Figures 2.8–2.9.

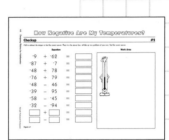

Figure 2.7

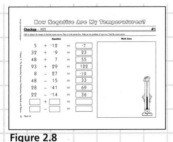

Figure 2.8

Figure 2.9

CHALLENGE ACTIVITY

The Integer Challenge graphic organizer (see Figure 2.10) can be used as an optional activity for those students in need of a bigger challenge. The challenge is in solving equations involving adding and subtracting fraction integers and decimal integers. A key to the challenge is provided in Figure 2.11.

Figure 2.10

Figure 2.11

VISUAL DISPLAY

When all parts of the task have been completed, students should organize all the components on a visual display or poster. Comparing the display with the rubric gives students clear expectations for their performance.

— ∞ —

In Summary

Standards give focus to efforts. They provide a clear vision of what it is teachers want students to know and be able to do. Standards offer the target, and it is the teacher's job to point students in the desired direction and create tasks that result in a clear view of the bull's-eye.

How Negative Are My Temperatures?

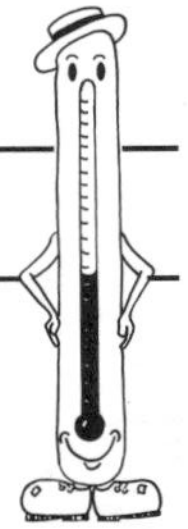

High and Low Temperature Record Organizer

Write the high and low record temperatures for each day of the month on the line provided. The third line for each day can be used to record the difference between the high and low temperatures.

_____ (month)

1 high ___ low ___ ___	**2** high ___ low ___ ___	**3** high ___ low ___ ___	**4** high ___ low ___ ___	**5** high ___ low ___ ___	**6** high ___ low ___ ___	**7** high ___ low ___ ___
8 high ___ low ___ ___	**9** high ___ low ___ ___	**10** high ___ low ___ ___	**11** high ___ low ___ ___	**12** high ___ low ___ ___	**13** high ___ low ___ ___	**14** high ___ low ___ ___
15 high ___ low ___ ___	**16** high ___ low ___ ___	**17** high ___ low ___ ___	**18** high ___ low ___ ___	**19** high ___ low ___ ___	**20** high ___ low ___ ___	**21** high ___ low ___ ___
22 high ___ low ___ ___	**23** high ___ low ___ ___	**24** high ___ low ___ ___	**25** high ___ low ___ ___	**26** high ___ low ___ ___	**27** high ___ low ___ ___	**28** high ___ low ___ ___
29 high ___ low ___ ___	**30** high ___ low ___ ___	**31** high ___ low ___ ___				

Figure 2.2

How Negative Are My Temperatures?

Adding and Subtracting Integers

Use this graphic organizer as a reminder of the procedures used to add and subtract integers.

Sign and Number	Operation	Signs and Number	Examples and Explanations

Positive Number

Negative Number

+

Positive Number

-

Positive Number

Negative Number

7 + 9 = 16
When both integers are positive, add as you add whole numbers.

15 + ⁻17 = ⁻2
In order to add a positive and negative integer, subtract the addend with the smaller absolute value from the addend with the higher absolute value. The answer takes the sign of the addend with the higher absolute value.

7 − 9 = 7 + ⁻9 = ⁻2
When subtracting positive integers, the subtraction sign becomes the sign of the second number and the operation sign becomes an addition sign. Since one number is now negative and the other positive, subtract the addend with the higher smaller absolute value from the addend with the higher absolute value. The answer takes the sign of the addend with the higher absolute value.

18 − ⁻24 = 18 + 24 = 42
Subtracting a negative number causes a double negative to occur. Both signs change to positive and the numbers are added to arrive at an answer.

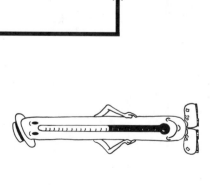

Figure 2.3

How Negative Are My Temperatures?

Adding and Subtracting Integers

Use this graphic organizer as a reminder of the procedures used to add and subtract integers.

Sign and Number   Operation   Signs and Number

Examples and Explanations

⁻7 + 9 = 2
In order to add a positive and negative integer, subtract the addend with the smaller absolute value from the addend with the higher absolute value. The answer takes the sign of the addend with higher absolute value.

⁻15 + ⁻17 = ⁻32
Since both integers are negative, the signs are the same so you add to find the answer. Because both signs are negative, the answer is negative.

⁻7 – 9 = ⁻7 + ⁻9 = ⁻16
When subtracting a negative integer from a negative integer, the subtraction sign becomes the sign of the second number and the operation sign becomes an addition sign. Since the integers are now the same sign, add to find the answer. The answer will be negative since both addends are negative.

⁻18 – ⁻24 = ⁻18 + 24 = 6
When subtracting a negative number from a negative number, a double negative occurs in front of the second integer. Those two signs change to positive. The integers' signs are now different. In order to add the positive and negative integers, subtract the addend with the smaller absolute value from the addend with the higher absolute value. The answer takes the sign of the addend with the higher absolute value.

Positive Number

Negative Number

Positive Number

Negative Number

+

–

Negative Number

Figure 2.4

How Negative Are My Temperatures?

Rubric

Instructions: Choose the point value that best describes the performance in each category.

	0 It's icy!	1 It's very cold!	2 It's getting warmer!	3 Perfect temperature!	Points Earned
Data Organizer Accuracy of Information	Not present or completely inaccurate	Half of the data missing or inaccurate	Data complete, some inaccuracies	Data complete and fully accurate	_____
Neatness	Sloppy, difficult to read	Can be read with careful concentration	Neat, easy to read	Perfectly formed numbers	_____
Accuracy of Answers Days 1–8	5–8 errors in calculations	3–4 errors in calculations	1–2 errors in calculations	Calculations perfect!	_____
Days 9–16	5–8 errors in calculations	3–4 errors in calculations	1–2 errors in calculations	Calculations perfect!	_____
Days 17–24	5–8 errors in calculations	3–4 errors in calculations	1–2 errors in calculations	Calculations perfect!	_____
Days 25–31	5–8 errors in calculations	3–4 errors in calculations	1–2 errors in calculations	Calculations perfect!	_____
Explanations Comparing Integers	Explanation missing	Explanation in need of clarification	Clear, accurate explanation	Clear, accurate explanation, includes examples	_____
Adding Integers	Explanation missing	Explanation in need of clarification	Clear, accurate explanation	Clear, accurate explanation, includes examples	_____
Subtracting Integers	Explanation missing	Explanation in need of clarification	Clear, accurate explanation	Clear, accurate explanation, includes examples	_____
Display	Lacks organization and neatness	Neatly organized, parts missing	Neatly organized, all components present	Neatly organized, attractive display, all components present	_____

Points possible = 30   Points earned = ____

Evaluator: _____

Figure 2.5

How Negative Are My Temperatures?

Checkup

Add or subtract the integers to find the correct answers. Place the answers in the boxes. Make up two problems of your own. Find the correct answers.

Equation

$$5 \quad + \quad {-12} \quad = \quad \boxed{}$$

$$32 \quad + \quad {-9} \quad = \quad \boxed{}$$

$$48 \quad + \quad 7 \quad = \quad \boxed{}$$

$$93 \quad + \quad 29 \quad = \quad \boxed{}$$

$$8 \quad - \quad 27 \quad = \quad \boxed{}$$

$$48 \quad - \quad 15 \quad = \quad \boxed{}$$

$$28 \quad - \quad {-41} \quad = \quad \boxed{}$$

$$22 \quad - \quad {-14} \quad = \quad \boxed{}$$

$$\boxed{} \quad + \quad \boxed{} \quad = \quad \boxed{}$$

$$\boxed{} \quad - \quad \boxed{} \quad = \quad \boxed{}$$

Work Area

Figure 2.6

How Negative Are My Temperatures?

Checkup

Add or subtract the integers to find the correct answers. Place the answers in the boxes. Make up two problems of your own. Find the correct answers.

Equation

-9 + -62 = ☐

-87 + -7 = ☐

-48 + 78 = ☐

-76 + 79 = ☐

-48 - 46 = ☐

-39 - 95 = ☐

-58 - -45 = ☐

-32 - -94 = ☐

☐ + ☐ = ☐

☐ - ☐ = ☐

Work Area

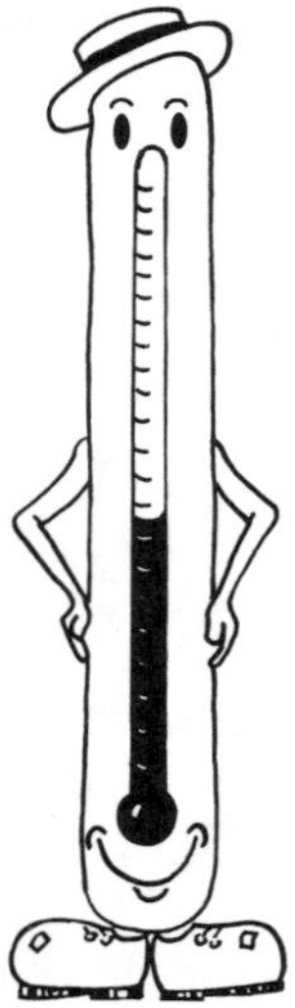

Figure 2.7

How Negative Are My Temperatures?

Checkup – Key   #1

Add or subtract the integers to find the correct answers. Place the answers in the boxes. Make up two problems of your own. Find the correct answers.

Equation

5	+	-12	=	-7
32	+	-9	=	23
48	+	7	=	55
93	+	29	=	122
8	–	27	=	-19
48	–	15	=	33
28	–	-41	=	69
22	–	-14	=	36
	+		=	
	–		=	

Work Area

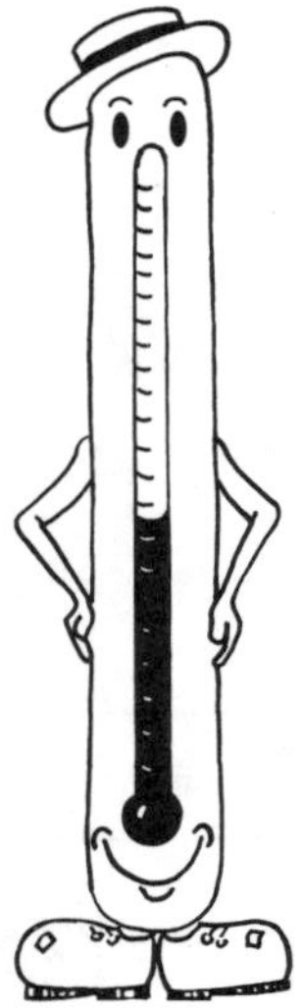

Figure 2.8

Chapter 2: The Relationship Between Mathematics Standards and Rubrics

Checkup – Key

Add or subtract the integers to find the correct answers. Place the answers in the boxes. Make up two problems of your own. Find the correct answers.

Equation

-9 + -62 = -71

-87 + -7 = -94

-48 + 78 = 30

-76 + 79 = 3

-48 - 46 = -94

-39 - 95 = -134

-58 - -45 = -13

-32 - -94 = 62

☐ + ☐ = ☐

☐ - ☐ = ☐

Work Area

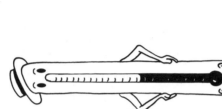

Figure 2.9

How Negative Are My Temperatures?

Integer Challenge

Solve each equation. Place your answer in the empty box.

-7.9	+		=	-48.3
	+	3.14	=	-7.02
-5.61	+	32	=	
38	+	-5.32	=	
-0.39	+		=	1

****

4.3	–		=	25
	–	-8.2	=	-41.3
	–	7.34	=	-2.03
-12.96	–		=	-17.39
	–	-34	=	-2.36

****

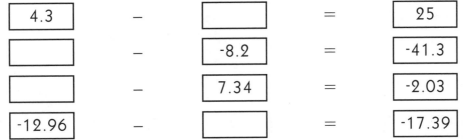

$-2\frac{1}{3}$	+	7	=	
	+	$4\frac{1}{2}$	=	$3\frac{3}{4}$
	+	$8\frac{9}{10}$	=	$-2\frac{2}{5}$
$4\frac{2}{7}$	+		=	$-8\frac{2}{3}$
$19\frac{1}{3}$	+		=	-27

****

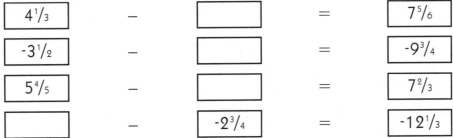

$4\frac{1}{3}$	–		=	$7\frac{5}{6}$
$-3\frac{1}{2}$	–		=	$-9\frac{3}{4}$
$5\frac{4}{5}$	–		=	$7\frac{2}{3}$
	–	$-2\frac{3}{4}$	=	$-12\frac{1}{3}$
	–	$8\frac{7}{8}$	=	$17\frac{1}{4}$

Figure 2.10

How Negative Are My Temperatures?

Integer Challenge – Key

Solve each equation. Place your answer in the empty box.

-7.9	+	**-40.4**	=	-48.3
-10.16	+	3.14	=	-7.02
-5.61	+	32	=	**26.39**
38	+	-5.32	=	**32.68**
-0.39	+	**1.39**	=	1

****

4.3	–	**-20.7**	=	25
-49.5	–	-8.2	=	-41.3
5.31	–	7.34	=	-2.03
-12.96	–	**4.43**	=	-17.39
-36.36	–	-34	=	-2.36

****

$-2\frac{1}{3}$	+	7	=	$4\frac{2}{3}$
$-\frac{3}{4}$	+	$4\frac{1}{2}$	=	$3\frac{3}{4}$
$-11\frac{3}{10}$	+	$8\frac{9}{10}$	=	$-2\frac{2}{5}$
$4\frac{2}{7}$	+	$-12\frac{20}{21}$	=	$-8\frac{2}{3}$
$19\frac{1}{3}$	+	$-46\frac{1}{3}$	=	-27

****

$4\frac{1}{3}$	–	$-3\frac{1}{2}$	=	$7\frac{5}{6}$
$-3\frac{1}{2}$	–	$6\frac{1}{4}$	=	$-9\frac{3}{4}$
$5\frac{4}{5}$	–	$-1\frac{13}{15}$	=	$7\frac{2}{3}$
$-15\frac{1}{12}$	–	$-2\frac{3}{4}$	=	$-12\frac{1}{3}$
$26\frac{1}{8}$	–	$8\frac{7}{8}$	=	$17\frac{1}{4}$

Figure 2.11

SkyLight Professional Development

Performance Tasks and Rubrics

Why Use Performance Tasks?

A performance task is a meaningful measurement of a student's level of understanding of a concept or concepts. Performance tasks relate knowledge to real-world applications. To complete a performance task, students are expected to use their computational skills to reason, communicate, and understand, not to simply reproduce memorized skills and procedures. According to Burke (1999), the key characteristic of performance tasks involves creating real-life applications for real-life problems. With performance tasks, students are asked to apply the skills and concepts they have learned to solving a problem, which helps to embed what they have learned. As Burke states, "By demonstrating what they can do, students have a greater probability of transferring the skills they learned to life rather than merely reproducing knowledge for a test" (79).

Students learn by being actively engaged in the learning process; they learn by doing (Zemelman, Daniels, and Hyde 1993). In mathematics, this equates to activities such as completing real-world tasks, collecting and analyzing data, and drawing conclusions from discoveries. Giving students the opportunity to perform complex tasks through such real-world applications gives educators new insights into what students really are able to do with the skills and knowledge they possess (Caudell 1996). Performance tasks also help students develop the ability to understand the relationships between concepts and procedures.

Students learn mathematical concepts by working with others to develop solutions to problems and by communicating their ideas and understandings. Such active engagement fosters metacognition and reflection while students are engaged in the task, which helps students better learn the concepts. The more often students engage in a concept, the better they become at that concept and the more likely they are to remember it. This is important because students need to make sense of the concepts in order to truly understand mathematical procedures. If students simply follow rules and copy down formulas established by others, they are not likely to develop the conceptual structure and reasoning skills needed to apply mathematical knowledge to real-world situations (Battista 1999).

The challenge for teachers is to provide students with opportunities to build mathematical confidence within the classroom so that students discover mathematics and its usefulness. As Crosswaite (1989) states, mathematics is not a spectator sport; active involvement is the key to understanding.

Black and Wiliam (1998) believe that to support the development of meaningful mathematical tasks, teaching and learning must be interactive and include the following characteristics:

- The development of tasks needs to be clearly tied to the learning aims or standards.

- Students must be provided the opportunity to communicate their evolving understandings during the implementation and developmental stages of a task.
- All students need to have the opportunity to express their ideas, and students need to be encouraged and involved in the thinking process.

Characteristics of Performance Tasks

When developing a performance task, the first thing teachers should keep in mind is that it is imperative that any performance task be directly linked to the standards and benchmarks being addressed. The focus of the task should be clear and expectations should be high. The purpose of the task should be accomplished through its performance.

The next thing teachers should consider is how the task relates to the real world. The task needs to have a real-world connection—it should go beyond isolated calculations and form a bridge between the concepts and their use in everyday life. Problems should be able to be generalized to other situations, and the problem's authenticity should also be apparent. The following questions can help ensure performance task has a real-world connection:

- Does the task actively engage the learner (i.e., will the learner conduct action research or participate in a hands-on activity to find the solution)?
- Will the task interest the students and does it have connections to their lives?
- Does the task promote higher-level thinking (i.e., does it require students to apply knowledge in a creative way)?
- Is there more than one correct answer to the task?

In addition to these characteristics, a real-world performance task should assess higher levels of understanding. The task should provide evidence that students can complete tasks requiring complex thinking processes (Schurr, Thomason, and Thomason 1996).

The scoring system for a performance task is unique and focuses on the task in comparison to the performance. A performance task does not have a single correct answer and cannot be evaluated like a traditional multiple-choice test, because it is more complex than a traditional test. With such tasks, students often find multiple ways to demonstrate their understanding and produce the information needed to create a solution. A rubric is the perfect evaluation tool for this type of performance.

Creating the Performance Task

There are several steps teachers can use as guidelines for creating a performance task.

Step 1: Choose the standards, benchmarks, and concepts that the task will measure. Doing this outlines the expected outcomes. When outlining such outcomes, keep the following questions in mind:

- What knowledge should students discover while they are performing the task?
- What skills are necessary to complete the performance?
- What accomplishments are necessary for the task to be considered a success?

Step 2: Develop a situation or real-world connection. Provide a task description in writing when developing the task. Consider the following questions:

- How are the mathematical concepts used in real life?
- What kind of task can extend students' knowledge and encourage mathematical connections to the world outside of the textbook?
- What procedures can actively engage students in a learning experience that puts their skills to use while engaging their brain in extensions of actual mathematical applications?

Step 3: Clearly outline the task by listing suggested procedures for task completion. During this process, keep in mind what students need to do to successfully complete the task.

List the supplies or tools needed for task implementation. It is important to keep costs reasonable; many tasks may not require additional supplies. To make sure all potential supplies are being considered, ask the following questions:

- Are special materials needed that are not typically found in the classroom?
- Who will purchase the items needed?
- Is access to a computer lab essential?

Step 4: Develop a time frame. Some tasks require a class period or two to complete, while more extensive tasks can take a few weeks. Make sure that the time commitment is justifiable, considering the concepts being addressed. When developing a time frame, consider the following:

- What is a reasonable length of time for task completion?
- Will the task be completed at school or will the task require time outside of the school day as well?

Step 5: Create a rubric. To create a rubric that fits the task, consider the following questions:

- What criteria are important to the successful completion of the task?
- What does an exemplary level of performance look like?

The Performance Task Planning Guide offered in Figure 3.1 provides an organizer that can be used to determine that all facets are addressed during task development.

— ∞ —

Performance Task Planning Guide

STANDARDS AND BENCHMARKS

MATHEMATICS CONCEPTS

TASK DESCRIPTION

SUGGESTED PROCEDURES

SUPPLIES AND SPECIAL NEEDS

TIME FRAME

ASSESSMENT TOOL

Figure 3.1

RUBRIC/MATHEMATICS
APPLICATION   Let's Go Shopping!

The rubric/mathematics application in this chapter centers on whole number and decimal operations. The real-world application, in this case, is shopping. From the time children are quite young, they realize that money is a necessary commodity if they want to obtain something. In school, they learn to add, subtract, multiply, and divide. This task turns students into consumers. They are given a budget and a purpose. It is their job to spend money responsibly, account for what they spend, and buy with a purpose. Students enjoy this task because they can shop and "spend money" at no cost.

An overview of the application is provided in Figure 3.2.

PERFORMANCE TASK EXPLANATION

Students are "given" $42 to spend on each family member for an upcoming event or holiday. Students who have small families might want to include extended family members. Students with large families may want to make purchases for a limited number of people. Three to eight members works well depending on the age level of the students completing the task. This task takes about two to three 45-minute class periods to complete. A task explanation that can be given to students is provided in Figure 3.3.

Figure 3.3

Using a variety of catalogs and newspaper ads, students should find gifts for each family member. Pictures of each gift should be neatly cut out and glued onto a gift display page. Each gift should be labeled with the price and the name of the family member to whom it will belong. A sample of the gift display page is shown in Figure 3.4.

Time limits will probably be needed for this part of the activity. Students will find they like to shop, and without some time structure, this part of the performance task could go on for a long time. Giving students one class period to shop is a good option. Encourage discussion during the gift selection process. Ask students to share their shopping strategies, discuss how they intend to spend their money, and compare prices with others in the class. All of these discussions are learning experiences for the students.

Upon completion of the gift display page, students should determine the total amount spent for each family member by filling out the Level 1 Receipt and

Figure 3.4

▪ UNIT OVERVIEW ▪
Let's Go Shopping!

STANDARDS Numbers and Operations, Problem Solving, Communication, Connections

MATHEMATICS CONCEPTS Whole number and decimal operations

GRADE LEVELS 3 through 9

RELATED CURRICULAR AREAS Art—Creating a display page; Language Arts—Writing an explanation

MATERIALS NEEDED Catalogs and newspaper ads

TASK Your family has a large celebration coming up and you need to buy gifts for everyone. You have been given a total of $42 per person to spend. You want to make sure that everyone gets at least 2 items.

SUGGESTED STUDENT PROCEDURES

1. Using catalogs and ads, find gifts for your family members (including yourself). Buy at least 2 gifts per person, spending as close to $42 for each person as possible.
2. Cut out pictures of each item you want to purchase. Create a display of each item and its price. Indicate which family member the gift is for.
3. For each family member, create a receipt, including an item description and price, as well as the total spent for that person.
4. Determine the total amount spent on gifts.
5. Complete the reflections page.
6. Make a folder or cover to hold your project. Include the gift display page, the receipts and calculations page, the reflections page, the rubric, and your checklist.

TEACHER RESOURCES

Task Explanation and Suggested Procedure page
Sample Gift Display
Receipt and Calculations page, Levels 1 and 2
Reflections page and Sample Key

Rubric
Checklist

INTERNET RESOURCES

FunBrain: Students can take part in an interactive Math Baseball game involving addition, subtraction, multiplication, and division, or all of these. <www.funbrain.com/math/>
A+ Math: This site helps students improve their mathematics skills interactively by offering flash cards, games, homework helpers, and worksheets. <http://www.aplusmath.com>
Do Math . . . and you can do anything: This site contains activities involving real-life mathematics challenges for students and families. <http://www.domath.org>

Figure 3.2

58

SkyLight Professional Development

Calculations page (see Figure 3.5). To make the task more difficult, teachers can use the Level 2 Receipt and Calculations form (see Figure 3.6), which asks students to calculate the tax for each individual item purchased.

Figure 3.5

All computations should be written on the form. Since one purpose of this activity is to increase computational skills, calculators should be avoided. Partner checking is an option to increase computational accuracy. To calculate the total amount spent, students can add together the money spent on each individual member. More than one copy of the receipts and calculations sheet will be needed for each student so they can include the information for all of their family members. To calculate the total budget, students can multiply the number of family members by \$42. By subtracting the total spent from the total budget, students determine the amount of money remaining.

The Reflections page (see Figure 3.7) can be completed as students finish other portions of the task. The reflections page helps students to embed their learnings by asking them to reflect on and consider the choices they made. An example of a student response to this reflection page is provided in Figure 3.8. After completing the reflection, students can create a cover for their work using a folder to organize and house the completed items.

Figure 3.6

Figure 3.7

Figure 3.8

RUBRIC

Distribute the rubric (see Figure 3.9) with the task explanation and suggested procedures. The performance task needs to be clearly explained, and the rubric is an aid to understanding. Direct students to look at the criteria in the left-hand column of the rubric. Read the descriptors for the 3-point column to make students aware of the level of expected quality. Students can refer to the rubric throughout the process for a reminder of the level of quality they should be working toward.

Figure 3.9

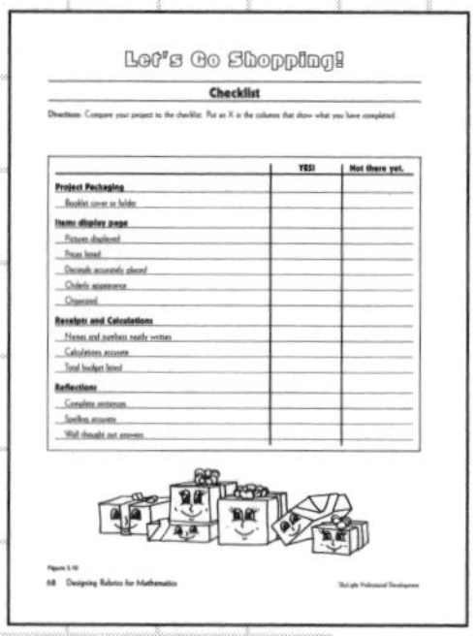

Let's Go Shopping!

Checklist

Directions: Compare your project to the checklist. Put an X in the column that show what you have completed.

	YES!	Not there yet.
Project Packaging		
Booklet cover or folder		
Items display page		
Pictures displayed		
Prices listed		
Decimals accurately placed		
Orderly appearance		
Organized		
Receipts and Calculations		
Names and numbers neatly written		
Calculations accurate		
Total budget listed		
Reflections		
Complete sentences		
Spelling accurate		
Well thought out answers		

Figure 3.10

Figure 3.10

CHECKLIST

Students can use the checklist in Figure 3.10 to determine if they have finished all the necessary steps for successful task completion before turning in their projects. This checklist contains many of the same criteria found in the rubric.

— ∞ —

In Summary

Performance tasks can be a catalyst for understanding. Skill repetition results in memorization, while performance tasks inspire thinking. Relating mathematics to real-world applications is a constructive way to bring purpose to the mathematics classroom and to help students apply their mathematics skills to solve real problems. Actively engaging students in learning helps them form connections and transfer their skills to new situations, which results in the meaningful use of skills and the extension of in-depth knowledge.

Let's Go Shopping!

Task Explanation and Suggested Procedures

Task:

Your family has a large celebration coming up and you need to buy gifts for everyone. You have been given $42 per person to spend. You want to make sure that everyone gets at least 2 items.

Suggested Procedures:

1. Using catalogs and ads, find gifts for your family members (including yourself). Buy at least 2 gifts per person, spending as close to $42 for each person as possible.

2. Cut out pictures of each item you want to purchase. Create a display including each item and its price. Indicate which family member the gift is for.

3. For each family member, create a receipt, including an item description and price, as well as the total spent for that person.

4. Determine the total amount spent on gifts.

5. Complete the reflections page.

6. Make a folder or cover to hold your project. Include the gift display page, the receipts and calculations page, the reflections page, the rubric, and your checklist.

Figure 3.3

Let's Go Shopping!

Sample Gift Display

Gifts for Dad

Place Picture
of Gift

Place Picture
of Gift

Item
Price = _____

Item
Price = _____

Gifts for Mom

Place Picture
of Gift

Place Picture
of Gift

Item
Price = _____

Item
Price = _____

Place
Picture
of Gift

Item
Price = _____

Gifts for My Sister

Place Picture
of Gift

Place Picture
of Gift

Item
Price = _____

Item
Price = _____

Gifts for Grandma

Place Picture
of Gift

Place Picture
of Gift

Item
Price = _____

Item
Price = _____

Figure 3.4

Let's Go Shopping!

Receipts and Calculations   Level 1

Total Budget = _____

Family Member: _____

Item	Cost
Total	

Family Member: _____

Item	Cost
Total	

Family Member: _____

Item	Cost
Total	

Family Member: _____

Item	Cost
Total	

Family Member: _____

Item	Cost
Total	

Family Member	Amount Spent
Grand Total	

Figure 3.5

Let's Go Shopping!

Receipts and Calculations   Level 2

Total Budget = _____

Family Member: _____

Item	Cost	Tax	Total
		Total	

Family Member: _____

Item	Cost	Tax	Total
		Total	

Family Member	Amount Spent
Grand Total	

Let's Go Shopping!

Reflections

Choose one of the gifts you selected. Why did you decide to buy it?

_____

_____

_____

_____

What mathematical skills did you use to complete this project?

_____

_____

_____

_____

Did you compare prices from different catalogs or ads? What would be the benefit of making price comparisons?

_____

_____

_____

_____

What did you learn while completing this task?

_____

_____

_____

_____

Figure 3.7

Let's Go Shopping!

Reflections – Sample Key

Choose one of the gifts you selected. Why did you decide to buy it?

I thought my mom would like a wallet and it was on sale.

What mathematical skills did you use to complete this project?

I added and subtracted to find out how much I spent and the money I could still spend.

Did you compare prices from different catalogs or ads? What would be the benefit of making price comparisons?

Some things I couldn't compare because it was only in one ad. I did compare the toys, because they were in two ads, and I could save money by taking the cheaper price.

What did you learn while completing this task?

It's not easy to shop for everyone when you have a budget. You really need to watch what you spend your money on.

Figure 3.8

Let's Go Shopping!

Rubric

Instructions: Highlight the box for each category that best describes the performance. Add points together to determine the rubric score.

	0	**1**	**2**	**3**
Cover	Not present or incomplete	Complete	Complete, neat	Complete, neat, includes project task explanations
Items Display Page Pictures	Not present or incomplete	Complete	Complete, labeled with family's names	Complete, labeled with family's names, neat
Prices	Not present or incomplete	Complete	Complete, includes decimal point and $	Complete, includes decimal point and $, neatly written
Appearance	Sloppy	Lacks organization	Organized	Organized and attractive
Receipts and Calculations Names and Numbers	Not present	Incomplete	Complete	Complete and neatly written
Calculations	Not present or 3 or more incorrect	2 incorrect	1 incorrect	All correct
Budget	Not present	Inaccurate	Accurate	Accurate and clearly labeled
Reflections	Not present	Present	Present, well thought out answers	Present, well thought out answers, complete sentences, accurate spelling

Evaluator: _____   Points possible = 24   Points earned = _____

Figure 3.9

Let's Go Shopping!

Checklist

Directions: Compare your project to the checklist. Put an X in the columns that show what you have completed.

	YES!	Not there yet.
Project Packaging		
Booklet cover or folder		
Items display page		
Pictures displayed		
Prices listed		
Decimals accurately placed		
Orderly appearance		
Organized		
Receipts and Calculations		
Names and numbers neatly written		
Calculations accurate		
Total budget listed		
Reflections		
Complete sentences		
Spelling accurate		
Well thought out answers		

Figure 3.10

Developing the Rubric from a Checklist

The Checklist

In the world of education, a checklist is an educational shopping list that indicates what teachers are looking (or shopping) for in a student product or performance, the goal of the task presented to students, and what the requirements and expectations of the task are. Checklists are the first step in developing a rubric. The checklist is also a tool to be used by students upon completion of a project to determine whether or not they have completed all portions of the task. Although checklists do not necessarily speak to quality, they do give students a clear picture of what still needs to be completed before they give their project to the teacher. Although checklists can be used for grading, they do not have the same impact as rubrics since checklists do not measure the quality of the work as rubrics do.

Teachers can use benchmarks to discern which parts of the task are the most important and should be highlighted through the checklist. Benchmarks provide such guidance because they outline the criteria the district deems important and necessary for various subject areas. To create an appropriate checklist, teachers should first list the task criteria, making sure to include everything important to a successful task outcome. The checklist should create a visual reminder of all that is crucial in the final product, and should be based on observable criteria.

A checklist must include:

- a list of criteria or components that need to be included in a finished product;
- a column to indicate the student has included the component; and
- a column to indicate the student has yet to complete the component.

Although a checklist can be a valuable tool, it has limitations. The checklist indicates whether a benchmark has been addressed, but the checklist does not speak to quality, and quality is the ultimate goal. The main difference between a checklist and a rubric is that the rubric describes quality, while the checklist simply indicates whether a component has been included. A checklist reminds students what they are expected to include in a completed piece of work; a rubric gives students a clear picture of the expectations of an exemplary performance. In order for a simple checklist to evolve into a rubric, a transition must take place.

The Transition from Checklist to Rubric

The checklist provides clear criteria that are important to the completion of the task or performance. Using those criteria, the teacher can develop a rubric to evaluate quality and understanding. The criteria outlined in the checklist are expanded in the rubric to include various levels of performance. The rubric should include precise performance expectations and provide students with a description of what the performance looks like. Rubrics should clearly indicate expectations, state targets, and describe evaluation criteria.

The rubrics used in each rubric/mathematics application sections in each chapter of this book are analytic rubrics. These rubrics were designed to evaluate a product as part of the formative process. Holistic rubrics are more summative, are not easily used as part of the growth process, and are typically used as a final evaluation of a product or performance. As discussed in chapter 1, analytic rubrics tend to give students feedback that is specific to their tasks and can be incorporated into the development process as both learning and evaluation tools. Danielson (1997) recommends analytic rubrics for classroom use, instead of holistic rubrics, because of the feedback they provide. The feedback offered by analytic rubrics helps students improve their performance because it provides information regarding specific expectations and gives descriptors that clearly outline what is needed for a higher level of performance.

Three basic steps are necessary to create a rubric. **Step one** is developing the checklist. The checklist becomes the criteria used for the rubric. Figure 4.1 shows a commonly used format for a rubric.

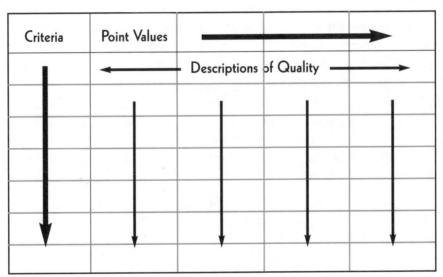

Figure 4.1

After listing the criteria, teachers need to make decisions regarding point value. Although the rubrics found within the Rubric/Mathematics Applications sections of this book are four-point rubrics, there is room for flexibility when creating point systems. However, there are some guidelines that teachers should consider during rubric development. If there are too many levels to a rubric, it becomes difficult to distinguish the difference between levels, and it also becomes increasingly complicated for students to use. If there are too few levels, room for growth or expansion within the levels may not be well represented.

Step two in creating a rubric is to develop the point scale for the rubric. An even number of points works well because there is no rubric middle, or center point. (With an odd number of points there is always a middle. For example, with 5 points, 3 is the middle point.) In rubric grading, teachers sometimes have a tendency to choose the center point value. If there is no center, teachers will use the descriptors more effectively, and the teacher will rely on the information stated for each level of the criteria.

After the point scale is chosen, teachers need to decide if a 0 or a 1 should be used as the lowest level of the rubric. In some cases, the lowest level of the rubric indicates little to no evidence of the expected criteria. In this case, a 0 may be more appropriate than a 1. (If the student showed little or no evidence of the expected criteria but received a 1 for these areas, the point total may not indicate that no evidence of the criteria was shown.) A 1 is typically used as the lowest level of the rubric when minimal evidence is shown that a student understands a concept or application component. Teachers also need to decide if the point value should be listed from lowest to highest or highest to lowest. The rubrics in this book list the point value from lowest to highest, as this allows students to see the point values as a step-by-step process that leads up to the ultimate performance. When rubrics are organized this way, the point values are written like building blocks, with each one building on the one before.

After point scale preferences are chosen, **step three** is to write descriptors for each level. It is imperative that descriptors be clear and precise and that the vocabulary used be appropriate to the age level of students who will be using, or who will be evaluated by, the rubric. Starting at the highest level of quality, expectations for each of the criterion should be described. Some questions teachers can consider when developing expectations include:

- How is an exemplary product or performance best described?
- What is the evidence of quality? (Be as specific as possible.)

Using previously completed student tasks can be helpful when determining levels of quality. These can be used as a guide or as a reminder as to which factors make up an exemplary performance and which factors constitute a lower score. Descriptors should not overlap from one level to the next, but rather should act as a step for each consecutive level. Descriptors often build on the previous level of performance, and this helps students and evaluators easily determine which level is an appropriate reflection of their products or performances.

While a rubric is a valuable tool that students can use as a guide to a higher level of quality, it is also a piece of work that is under construction. As the rubric is used, it will become apparent if editing is necessary, and adjustments can be made as necessary.

Summary of Steps for Developing a Rubric

The three basic steps for developing a rubric have been outlined in the previous paragraphs. The following figures provide a closer look at rubric development through each step in the process.

Step 1: Develop a checklist (see Figure 4.2) and develop rubric criteria from the checklist (see Figure 4.3).

The checklist in Figure 4.2 was developed for a graphing project and was developed from district benchmarks based on the NCTM standard "All students should select, create, and use appropriate graphical representations of data" (NCTM 2000, 248).

Checklist for a Rubric		
	YES!	**Not yet.**
Does the graph have a title?		
Does each axis have a label or title?		
Is the x-axis numbered accurately or is the proper information supplied?		
Is the y-axis numbered accurately?		
Is there a key present?		
Is the information graphed according to the key?		
Is the information graphed accurately?		

Figure 4.2

The rubric in Figure 4.3 is based on the geometry standard, and the benchmark deals with students' ability to design a graph. When developing the list of criteria or components, the teacher should keep in mind any and all components that need to be included for successful completion of the product. The criterion listed in this rubric corresponds to the benchmarks listed in the checklist in Figure 4.2.

Developing Rubric Criteria				
Does the graph have a title?				
Does each axis have a label or title?				
Is the x-axis numbered accurately or is the proper information supplied?				
Is the y-axis numbered accurately?				
Is there a key present?				
Is the information graphed according to the key?				
Is the information graphed accurately?				

Figure 4.3

Step 2: Develop the point system for each criterion (see Figure 4.4).

The next step in the process is to develop a point system for the rubric. It is important to use a point system that has enough descriptors to properly evaluate the product and few enough so that it is easy for students to use and understand.

Developing a Point System				
	0 ☐	**1** ☐	**2** ☐	**3** ☐
Does the graph have a title?				
Does each axis have a label or title?				
Is the x-axis numbered accurately or is the proper information supplied?				
Is the y-axis numbered accurately?				
Is there a key present?				
Is the information graphed according to the key?				
Is the information graphed accurately?				

Figure 4.4

Step 3: Develop the descriptors for each level of quality (see Figure 4.5).

Once a point system is in place, a descriptor for each level of quality should be developed. Descriptors should be written using words that students are familiar with. In order for the rubric to affect student performance, students must be able to understand it. Descriptors for the highest level of quality should be developed first. This indicates a top-notch performance and describes the highest level of quality. The developer can then work backward from that point, deciding which criteria make up the descending point values. Once all the descriptors have been filled in, the rubric is complete and ready to use.

	0	**1**	**2**	**3**
Does the graph have a title?	Not titled	Partially or inaccurately titled	Title present but with errors	Titled accurately
Does each axis have a label or title?	Not titled	Titles present but inappropriate	Titles present but with errors	Titled accurately
Is the x-axis numbered accurately or is the proper information supplied?	Not labeled or numbered	Label or numbers present but inappropriate	Label or numbers present but with errors	Labeled or numbered accurately
Is the y-axis numbered accurately?	Not labeled or numbered	Label or numbers present but inappropriate	Label or numbers present but with errors	Labeled or numbered accurately
Is there a key present?	Not present	Present but incomplete	Present with inaccuracies	Present and accurate
Is the information graphed according to the key?	No correspondance	Much graphed inaccurately	Graphed with minor error	Graphed according to the key
Is the information graphed accurately?	Graph incomplete	Graph complete with several errors	Graph complete with 1–2 errors	Graph complete and accurate

Figure 4.5

— ∞ —

RUBRIC/MATHEMATICS
APPLICATION   What's My Area?

The following rubric/mathematics application allows students to extend their geometric knowledge by finding the area of an unusual shape. This application contains a checklist and a rubric. A comparison of the two demonstrates how a checklist can be used as a foundational piece for a rubric. An overview of the application is offered in Figure 4.6.

PERFORMANCE TASK EXPLANATION
Students create an unusual shape of their own and find its area. During this process it will become obvious to students that by dividing an unusual shape into smaller geometric shapes the area can be computed with relative ease. This task helps students extend their knowledge of the use of formulas in finding area to a higher level of performance. This task can typically be completed in four 45-minute periods for a fifth or sixth grade class—less time is needed for older students and more time for younger students.

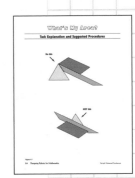

Figure 4.7

Students draw and cut out a combination of eight rectangles, triangles, parallelograms, and trapezoids from various colors of construction or brightly colored paper. Shapes are glued onto a large piece of poster paper. Sides of the shapes should be aligned, but not overlapping (see Figure 4.7). Students measure and number each shape for identification purposes. They need to determine the location of the base and height of each shape and measure each to the nearest centimeter. Measurements should be accurately recorded on each shape. For organizational purposes, students should record all necessary information on the chart provided in Figure 4.8.

Figure 4.8

The area of each individual shape should be calculated. After finding the areas of each shape, students add the areas together to discover the area of their creations. To provide evidence of understanding, students should write an explanation of the process they used to find the entire area. That process should be related to the original problem of finding the area of an unusual shape.

To make the task cohesive and organized, all information should be neatly placed on a poster board or piece of construction paper. Information should be sensibly organized in a logical fashion so that anyone looking at the poster can determine the

▪ UNIT OVERVIEW ▪
What's My Area?

STANDARDS Measurement, Problem Solving, Communication, Connections

MATHEMATICS CONCEPTS Area of rectangles, triangles, parallelograms, and trapezoids

GRADE LEVELS 2 through 10

RELATED CURRICULAR AREAS Language Arts—Writing explanations; Art—Creating a poster

MATERIALS NEEDED Assorted colors of construction paper, scissors, glue, poster board or large construction paper, rulers

TASK Andre Pentagon, a popular architect, creates houses with unusual shapes. He combines various geometric shapes to create unique rooms. This is a problem for the carpet layers who are working on his current house. They do not know how to calculate the area of the house and cannot determine the amount of carpeting needed. You need to teach the carpet layers how to determine the area of these unusual houses.

SUGGESTED STUDENT PROCEDURES

Create an unusual shape comprised of a variety of geometric shapes. Combine rectangles, triangles, parallelograms, and trapezoids. Follow the procedures listed.

1. Choose eight or more pieces of construction paper no smaller than 12cm by 12cm each.
2. Using scissors and a ruler, draw and cut 2 rectangles, 2 triangles, 2 parallelograms, and 2 trapezoids. Each shape should have different dimensions.
3. Number each shape. Measure the base and height of each shape to the nearest centimeter. Write the measurement in the appropriate location on each shape.
4. Align the sides of the shapes in any layout desired. Do not overlap shapes. Glue the pieces onto construction paper to create one large shape out of the smaller pieces.
5. Find the area of each individual shape using the measurements and the proper formulas. Find the area of the larger shape. Use the chart provided to record all information.
6. Write an explanation of the process used to find the area of the irregular shape created. Include an explanation regarding how this applies to the work of the carpet layers.
7. Organize your work on a poster. Include the shape created, the chart, and an explanation of the procedures used.

TEACHER RESOURCES

Example Shape page
Organizational Chart
Project Layout Example
Task Explanation and
    Suggested Procedures page
Rubric
Student Helper
Checkup and Key

INTERNET RESOURCES

Interactive Mathematics Miscellany and Puzzles: Features information on mathematics including logic games and puzzles, proofs, web polls, and links to other mathematics sites. <http://www.cut-the-knot.com/content.html>
Math Pop Quiz: Cool quiz network site that includes quizzes on complementary, supplementary, corresponding, and exterior angles. <http://www.mathpopquiz.com>
Professor's Freedman's Math Tips: Mathematics strategies for teacher and students including ways to help students deal with mathematics anxiety, study skills and fun resources. <http://www.mathpower.com>

Figure 4.6
78

SkyLight Professional Development

information and procedures used to find the area of the irregular shape created by the student (see Figure 4.9 for an example).

Figure 4.9

Figure 4.10

RUBRIC

The rubric (Figure 4.10) should be distributed to students before the task begins. This makes students aware of the task expectations before beginning the performance task. The Task Explanation and Suggested Procedures page (see Figure 4.11) can also be distributed at this time. It provides students with a copy of the problem as well as suggested procedures for accomplishing the task. The problem and procedures should be discussed and questions answered. Flexibility is important; if necessary, procedures should be adjusted to meet the needs of students.

Figure 4.11

The rubric used for this task is based on a four-point scale and is a weighted rubric, which means that concepts or performances viewed as more crucial to the understanding of the task are given additional value or weight. (For more information on weighted rubrics, see chapter 5.) For an example of how to determine scores on a weighted rubric, look at the calculations category on the rubric in Figure 4.11. It has a weight of x 3. If a student earns 2 points in this category, the points are multiplied by the value of three. Therefore, the student earns 6 points in this category.

Taking a few minutes of class time to highlight the highest expectations results in products of elevated quality. The four-point section on the rubric should be clear to the students so they aim for the top level of achievement. In the case of a weighted rubric, students should also be aware of the weight that corresponds to each criterion.

When tasks are finished and the individual scores for each rubric criterion have been determined, simply add all the individual scores together. If it is necessary to turn the rubric score into a percent, divide the points earned by the total points possible. The grading scale will vary depending on class procedures. Students should be encouraged to self- and peer-assess before turning in their projects to the teacher. It is beneficial to give students the opportunity to improve scores after the rubric has been completed. This practice heightens student performance and level of achievement.

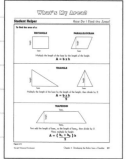

Figure 4.12

STUDENT HELPER

Students may be given a copy of the Student Helper tool (see Figure 4.12). This worksheet helps students identify the proper formula when finding the individual areas.

EXPANDING THE TASK

Expanding the performance task can be accomplished in any way that fits the mathematics curriculum being taught. For example, students can find the area of circles; squares; obtuse, acute, scalene, and isosceles triangles; and so forth. The number of shapes used can be increased to add to the level of difficulty. Students can also brainstorm their own procedures and create their own organizational tools to complete the task.

SIMPLIFYING THE TASK

The performance task can be simplified for younger students by limiting the types of geometric shapes used to one or two. Students might use only rectangles, for example. In this case, each rectangle should be of different dimensions.

CHECKUP

This optional activity is designed to be used as an assessment. This activity is modeled after the original task but has an increased level of difficulty. In the assessment provided in Figure 4.13, students are asked to find the area of an unusual shape, which is comprised of a combination of trapezoids, rectangles, parallelograms, and triangles. Students are only able to see the outline of the unusual shape and must divide it into geometric shapes, make the appropriate measurements, and create an organizational tool to record the information needed to complete the task. This chart can be similar to the one used in the students' original task and should include formulas, measurements, calculations, and total area.

Figure 4.13

For some students, this task may be quite difficult. If simplification is required, assist students when they divide the unusual shape or create the divisions before duplicating the assessment for students. The divisions can be drawn on the master copy.

An answer key is located on Figure 4.14. Students may find other ways to divide the shape, but the total area should be within a few centimeters of the area provided on the answer key.

— ∞ —

Figure 4.14

80

In Summary

The first step in creating a rubric is to create a checklist. The checklist should clearly state the criteria crucial to the task. After determining the point values, descriptors should be created that illustrate each level of performance. Finally, the rubric is put to the test by trying it with students. Rubrics can always be considered "under construction"—teachers should adjust them as necessary to meet their needs and the needs of their students.

What's My Area?

Do this

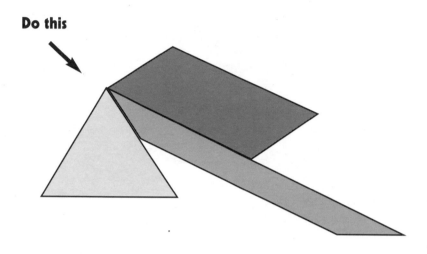

NOT this

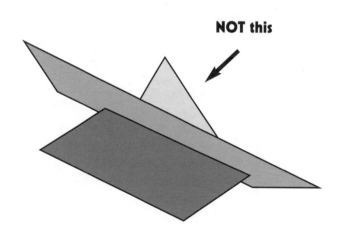

Figure 4.7

What's My Area?

Organizational Chart

Instructions: Complete the chart using the shapes and measurements from the unusual shape you created.

Number and Shape	Formula	Measurements in Formula	Calculations	Area

Total Area = _____

Figure 4.8

What's My Area?

Project Layout Example

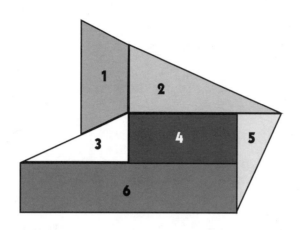

Number and Shape	Formula	Measurements in Formula	Calculations	Area
1. trapezoid	$\left(\dfrac{b_1+b_2}{2}\right)h = A$			
2. triangle	$\dfrac{b \times h}{2} = A$			
3. triangle	$\dfrac{b \times h}{2} = A$			
4. rectangle	$b \times h = A$			
5. triangle	$\dfrac{b \times h}{2} = A$			
6. rectangle	$b \times h = A$			

Total Area = _____

Explanation: In order to find the area of the total shape, it was necessary to find the area of each individual shape using the proper formulas and measurements. After finding the area of each shape, I added the six areas together to arrive at the area of the unusual shape.

If the carpet layers need to find the area of an unusually shaped house, they should first divide the house into shapes they are able to find the area of. Using the proper formulas they can find the areas of the individual units then add them together to find the area of the house.

Figure 4.9

What's My Area?

Rubric

Instructions: Determine which description best fits the completed task for every category on the rubric. Place the earned point value on the line in the last column and multiply by the weight to compute each score. Add scores together to calculate the final score.

	1	2	3	4	
Geometric Shapes Shapes	A combination of 1–3 rectangles, triangles, trapezoids, and parallelograms present and neatly numbered	A combination of 4–5 rectangles, triangles, trapezoids, and parallelograms present and neatly numbered	A combination of 6–7 rectangles, triangles, trapezoids, and parallelograms present and neatly numbered	A combination of 8 or more rectangles, triangles, trapezoids, and parallelograms present and neatly numbered	____ × 2 = ____
Base and height	1–3 shapes have the base and height accurately and neatly labeled	4–5 shapes have the base and height accurately and neatly labeled	6–7 shapes have the base and height accurately and neatly labeled	8 or more shapes have the base and height accurately and neatly labeled	____ × 2 = ____
Organizational Chart Shapes named and numbered	1–3 shapes are accurately numbered and identified by name on the chart	4–5 shapes are accurately numbered and identified by name on the chart	6–7 shapes are accurately numbered and identified by name on the chart	8 or more shapes are accurately numbered and identified by name on the chart	____ × 1 = ____
Formulas	1–3 formulas are present and accurate for the corresponding shape	4–5 formulas are present and accurate for the corresponding shape	6–7 formulas are present and accurate for the corresponding shape	8 or more formulas are present and accurate for the corresponding shape	____ × 2 = ____
Calculations	1–3 calculations are present and accurate for the corresponding shape	4–5 calculations are present and accurate for the corresponding shape	6–7 calculations are present and accurate for the corresponding shape	8 or more calculations are present and accurate for the corresponding shape	____ × 3 = ____
Area	1–3 areas correctly computed and labeled with the square unit	4–5 areas correctly computed and labeled with the square unit	6–7 areas correctly computed and labeled with the square unit	8 or more areas correctly computed and labeled with the square unit	____ × 1 = ____
Written Explanation	Difficult to understand	Clearly written, contains 3 or more spelling or grammatical errors	Clearly written, contains 1–2 spelling or grammatical errors	Clearly written, perfect spelling and punctuation	____ × 2 = ____
Poster or Display	Incomplete or lacking neatness	Complete, neat	Complete, neat, and organized	Complete, well organized, and attractive	____ × 1 = ____

Evaluator: _____   Points possible = 56   Points earned = ____

Figure 4.10

What's My Area?

Task Explanation and Suggested Procedures

Task:

Andre Pentagon, a popular architect, creates houses with unusual shapes. He combines various geometric shapes to create rooms unlike any others. This has created a problem for the carpet layers who are working on his current house. They do not know how to calculate the area of the house and are unable to determine the amount of carpeting needed. Your help is needed. You need to teach the carpet layers how to determine the area of these unusual houses.

Suggested Procedures:

Create an unusual shape comprised of a variety of geometric shapes. Use a combination of rectangles, triangles, parallelograms and trapezoids. Follow the procedures listed.

1. Choose 8 or more pieces of construction paper no smaller than 12cm x 12cm each.

2. Using scissors and a ruler, draw and cut 2 rectangles, 2 triangles, 2 parallelograms, and 2 trapezoids. Each shape should have different dimensions.

3. Number each shape. Measure the base and height of each shape to the nearest centimeter. Write the measurement in the appropriate location on each shape.

4. Align the sides of the shapes in any layout desired. Do not overlap shapes. Glue the pieces onto construction paper to create one large shape out of the smaller pieces.

5. Find the area of each individual shape using the measurements and the proper formulas. Find the area of the larger shape. Use the chart provided to record all information.

6. Write an explanation of the process used to find the area of the irregular shape created. Include an explanation as to how this applies to the work of the carpet layers.

7. Organize your work on a poster. Include the shape created, the chart, and explanation of the procedures used.

Figure 4.11

What's My Area?

To find the area of a:

RECTANGLE   ### PARALLELOGRAM

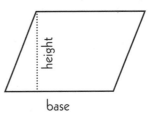

Multiply the length of the base by the length of the height.

$$A = b \times h$$

TRIANGLE

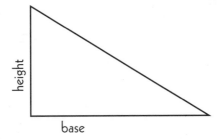
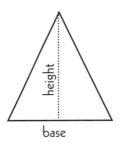

Multiply the length of the base by the length of the height, then divide by 2.

$$A = \frac{b \times h}{2}$$

TRAPEZOID

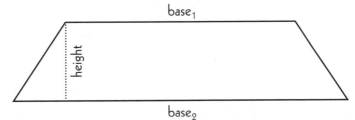

First add the length of base$_1$ to the length of base$_2$, then divide by 2.
Next, multiply by height.

$$A = \frac{(b_1 + b_2) \, h}{2}$$

Figure 4.12

What's My Area?

Find the area of the shape below. Place any necessary measurements directly on the shape. Measurements should be made to the nearest half of a centimeter (.5 cm). Create a chart to organize all information needed to find the area. Include all formulas, calculations, and areas used to determine the area of the unusual shape.

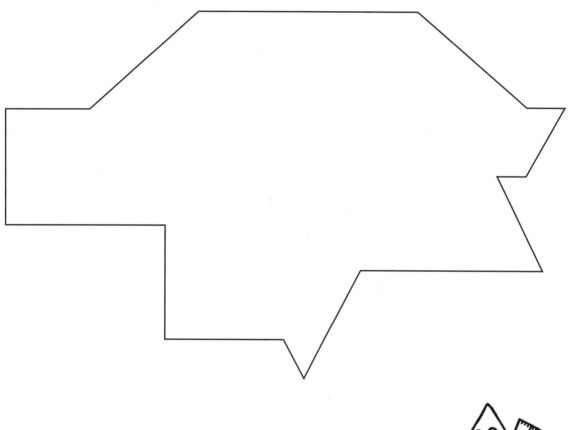

HINT: Remember the What's My Area? task. You might want to use similar strategies.

Figure 4.13

What's My Area?

Checkup – Key

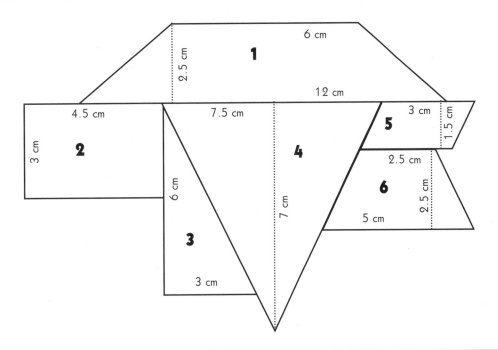

Number and Shape	Formula	Measurements in Formula	Calculations (work space)	Area
1. Trapezoid	$\left(\dfrac{b_1+b_2}{2}\right) h = A$	$\left(\dfrac{6+12}{2}\right) 2.5 = A$		22.5 cm²
2. Rectangle	$b \times h = A$	$4.5 \times 3 = A$		13.5 cm²
3. Triangle	$\dfrac{b \times h}{2} = A$	$\dfrac{3 \times 6}{2} = A$		9 cm²
4. Triangle	$\dfrac{b \times h}{2} = A$	$\dfrac{7.5 \times 7}{2} = A$		26.25 cm²
5. Parallelogram	$b \times h = A$	$3 \times 1.5 = A$		4.5 cm²
6. Trapezoid	$\left(\dfrac{b_1+b_2}{2}\right) h = A$	$\left(\dfrac{2.5+5}{2}\right) 2.5 = A$		9.375 cm²
			Total Area = 85.125 cm²	

Figure 4.14

Weighted Rubrics

The Purpose of Weighted Rubrics

Weighted rubrics are rubrics that give additional weight to concepts or performances thought to be more important to the task. This type of rubric uses multipliers to increase the value of specific criteria. When grading a piece of student work, it might become apparent that some criteria are more important than others, or some part of a performance is more crucial to understanding than another. When this is the case, a weighted rubric is of great value. For example, if neatness is a component that is important to the teacher, but not as important as the computational aspects of a task, a weighted rubric would be the solution. With a weighted rubric, students can easily see that some components are deemed more important than others and therefore know where to spend the majority of their time. Students respond well to the additional information that weighted rubrics provide. An example of a weighted rubric designed to evaluate a double bar or double line graph is provided in Figure 5.1.

Criteria	0 Points	1 Point	2 Points	3 Points	
Graph title	Not present	Present	• Present • Appropriate to topic	• Present • Appropriate to topic • Correct capitalization and spelling	___ x 2 = ___
Axes titles	Not present	Present	• Present • Appropriate to topic	• Present • Appropriate to topic • Correct capitalization and spelling	___ x 2 = ___
Numbering/Labeling x-axis	Inaccurate	Accurate	• Accurate • Well placed	• Accurate • Well placed • Easy to read	___ x 2 = ___
Numbering/Labeling y-axis	Inaccurate	Accurate	• Accurate • Well placed	• Accurate • Well placed • Easy to read	___ x 2 = ___
Data	Incomplete	Inaccurately graphed	Accurately graphed	• Accurately graphed • Neat	___ x 10 = ___
Key	Not present	Inaccurate	Accurate	• Accurate • Neat	___ x 2 = ___
Overall Neatness	Sloppy	Room for improvement	Neat	Perfect!	___ x 1 = ___

Name_____ Evaluator_____ Points Possible = 63 Points Earned = ___

Grading Scale: 57–63 = A 50–56 = B 43–49 = C 37–42 = D 36 and below = F

Figure 5.1

The criteria listed in the left-hand column of the figure are important to the successful completion of the graph, but perhaps they do not hold equal importance to each other. In the far right-hand column, a weight or point value multiplier is listed for each criteria. The criteria with a higher multiplier are deemed more crucial to the understanding of the task in comparison to the others. When selecting the weight to be used for each category, teachers need to decide the degree of importance placed on the criteria. Teachers should ask themselves, Is the category twice as important as others, five times as important, or more?

When creating a weighted rubric, teachers need not try to predetermine the amount of total rubric points. Point values for rubrics can vary. A 100-point scale is not needed to use percent grades. Teachers can begin to develop the weighted rubric by establishing the number of levels and the corresponding point value, creating the rubric, and determining the desired weights.

When using this rubric to evaluate a product, the teacher determines the point value that most appropriately fits each level of performance. The teacher then uses the multipliers to determine the final score in each category. For example, if totally accurate computations are worth 4 points, and the multiplier is worth 5 points, this criterion would be worth 20 on a project with perfect computations.

Individual scores for each criterion are added to reach the final rubric score. Teachers can calculate the total points possible by taking the highest point level on the rubric and multiplying that number by the sum of the multipliers. For example, the rubric in Figure 5.1 has a 3 as the highest level and its multipliers total 21. The total points possible on this rubric are calculated by multiplying 3 by 21, which equals 63 points. To determine a percent for a final rubric score, teachers should divide the points earned by the points possible and round to the nearest percent. It is important to remember that the percent calculated directly from the rubric might be low and might not fit into a traditional grading scale. Additional points may need to be added to create a fair grade. After all, a level 2 performance on the rubric in Figure 5.1 is an adequate performance, which might indicate a "B" or a "C" in a traditional grading system, but two out of three as a percent is only 66%. The chart in Figure 5.2 offers tips for turning the rubric percent into one that better fits a traditional grading system. (For more information on converting rubric scores to letter grades, see appendix 2.)

If the Rubric Percent Is Equal To:	Grades
88–100	A
75–87	B
62–74	C
50–61	D
0–50	F

Figure 5.2

Weighted rubrics are easy to create and useful when prioritizing criteria. To educators, the weighted rubric emphasizes quality in all areas of a product without sacrificing the opportunity to stress categories that might be more important to the mathematical understanding of the work.

Using Technology in Rubric Development

There are many ways that technology can be used to aid in the rubric development process. Teachers can start by locating their district's benchmarks on their district's Web site. Once this has been done and the teacher has developed a checklist, he or she can use a spreadsheet program, such as Microsoft Word (using text boxes), Excel, or the Rubricator to set up the rubric.

Technology can also be helpful for getting ideas for rubrics from educators and schools around the world. There are numerous Web sites devoted to rubrics; many offer rubrics that can be reproduced for classroom use. Typing the word *rubrics* in any of the major search engines (such as Yahoo!, HotBot, or AltaVista) will yield a large variety of such sites. However, just because a rubric is on the Web does not necessarily mean it is a quality rubric. Make sure to check rubrics for sensibility, clarity of descriptors, use of point values, applicability to standards, simplicity of language, and basic set-up (e.g., will it be easy to read and easy for students to understand?)

Some rubric sites and rubric-related sites that contain information on rubrics include:

1. **Rubrics for Web Lessons:** Contains links to articles about rubrics and authentic assessment, holistic rubrics for various topics, a rubric template, and other rubric resources.
   <http://edweb.sdsu.edu/triton/july/rubrics/Rubrics_for_Web_Lessons.html>

2. **Using Rubrics in Middle School:** Features tips for creating rubrics and examples of analytic rubrics for such areas as book reports, oral presentations, persuasive essays, and more.
   <http://www.middleweb.com/rubricsHG.html>

3. **Evaluation Rubrics for Web sites:** Includes rubrics that primary, intermediate and secondary grade students can use to evaluate Web sites on the Internet when conducting Internet research.
   <http://www.siec.k12.in.us/~west/online/eval.htm>

4. **Kathy Schrock's Guide for Educators—Assessment Rubrics:** Comprises a categorized, annotated list of over 1,600 sites to help educators, teachers, and parents enhance instruction and support the curriculum.
   <http://school.discovery.com/schrockguide/assess.html>

5. **Kid Language Writing Rubrics:** Contains analytic rubrics geared toward middle school students for topics such as writing to inform, writing to persuade, and writing for personal expression.
<http://www.intercom.net/local/school/sdms/mspap/kidwrit.html>

6. **Alternative Assessment in Geography:** Features holistic scoring rubrics for elementary, middle, and high school geography projects.
<http://www.coe.ilstu.edu/jabraun/socialstudies/assess/geo/samples/sam-k-01.html>

7. **Mother of All Rubrics:** Includes an analytic rubric teachers can use to assess their rubric evaluation.
<http://tiger.coe.missouri.edu/~arcwww/pa/olive.html>

8. **Evaluation Plan for Rubrics:** Features analytic rubrics for friendly letters and business letters, as well as student samples of both.
<http://volweb.utk.edu/Schools/bedford/harrisms/letterrubric.htm>

9. **All About Rubrics and Assessment:** Contains information on designing a rubric, samples of analytic rubrics, and a template for making problem-based learning checklists for various grade level and topics.
<http://expage.com/page/lebeaurubrics>

10. **Assessment Rubric Links:** Comprises links to Web sites with rubrics for assessing various multimedia projects.
<http://www.forsyth.k12.ga.us/jhobson/multimed.htm>

11. **The Staff Room for Ontario's Teachers:** Offers sample rubrics for many topics, including everything from dance to technology to foreign languages. Also features links to online rubric and checklist creation sites.
<http://www.odyssey.on.ca/%7Eelaine.coxon/rubrics.htm>

— ∞ —

RUBRIC/MATHEMATICS APPLICATION
Discoveries in Rainbow Candy Land

In the following rubric/mathematics application, students change fractions to decimals and then to percents to determine the percentage of various colored candies in a package. This application contains a weighted rubric that can be used to assess the task. An overview of the application is provided in Figure 5.3.

PERFORMANCE TASK EXPLANATION

This task helps students understand the relationship between fractions, decimals, and percentages. During completion of the task, students are expected to manipulate numbers from one form to another. Through performance and discussion, students learn that different forms of numbers can be used in different ways. Decimals and percents, for example, are better than fractions when used to compare two numbers.

Task procedures are described in the overview and in Figure 5.4. To begin the process, students need a fun size bag of colored candies (like M&M's). Using the data collection chart (see Figure 5.5) students record several pieces of information. Students can also be encouraged to create a data chart of their own. A sample that shows how students can use the data collection chart is provided in Figure 5.6.

This performance task can typically be completed in three 45-minute class periods. If calculators and computers are used to make a chart and list data, the project should take middle school students approximately two 45-minute class periods.

<u>Helpful Hint:</u> After giving the students the candy, have them open it and pour the contents into a clear zipper-type sandwich bag. When the bag is sealed, the

Figure 5.4

Figure 5.5

Figure 5.6

▪ UNIT OVERVIEW ▪
Discoveries in Rainbow Candyland

STANDARDS   Numbers and Operations, Data Analysis and Probability, Communication, Representation

MATHEMATICS CONCEPTS   Changing fractions to decimals to percents

GRADE LEVELS   4 through 9

RELATED CURRICULAR AREAS   Language Arts—Writing an explanation, writing a business letter

MATERIALS NEEDED   One package of fun size colored candies for each student or cooperative group

TASK   The Rainbow Candy Corporation has uncovered possible inconsistencies within their fun size packages of colored candies. Customers have been voicing their opinions about varying amounts of colors between packages. The research department is requesting your help. They need you to determine if the claims are accurate. They would also like a report of your findings.

SUGGESTED STUDENT PROCEDURES

1. Find out how many candies there are of each color. Write each number as a fraction of the total and as a decimal and a percent.
2. Organize the information on an easy-to-understand chart.
3. Explain how you arrived at your mathematical answers.
4. Share your findings with the class. Discuss class discoveries.
5. Write a letter to the Rainbow Candy Land Corporation sharing class findings. Include observations and recommendations.

TEACHER RESOURCES

Task Explanation and Suggested Procedures page
Data Collection Chart and Sample Key
Explanations and Examples form and Sample Key
Rubric
Fractions, Decimals, and Percents Checkup and Key

INTERNET RESOURCES

LightSpan: Provides mathematics study skills and tips, puzzles and problems, and links to articles and other Web sites. <http://www.lightspan.com>
SOS Math: This great study site for high school students provides mathematics review material ranging from algebra to differential equations. <http://www.sosmath.com>
Math League: This site offers information on mathematics contests for students in pre-kindergarten through high school, as well as sample contests and activities. <http://www.mathleague.com>

Figure 5.3

students can manipulate the candy without being concerned about the condition of their desktop or the cleanliness of their hands.

In the first column of the chart, students record the colors found in each package. Colors may not be the same for every student, as every color is not necessarily in every bag.

Figure 5.7

The second column should list the exact number of colored candies found of each color. Students then determine the total number of candies in each bag and create fractions to express the amount of each color compared to the total amount of candy. The numerator (top) of the fraction is the number specific to the color. The denominator (bottom) of the fraction is the total number of candies found in the package.

Next, students change the fractions into decimals and then into percents. To convert the fraction into a decimal, students divide the numerator by the denominator. To find the percent, students multiply the decimal by 100. (The percent can also be found by moving the decimal two places to the right). Calculators are an option at this point of the task, but if the purpose is to practice skills in dividing decimals, teachers may want to make this a paper-and-pencil exercise. Upon completion of each section of the chart, students should explain, in writing, the procedure used to arrive at answers. The Explanations and Examples form (see Figure 5.7) can be used for this purpose. Figure 5.8, which was completed by a student, shows an example of how a student might fill out this form.

Figure 5.8

While students are completing calculations, teachers should encourage discussion. Remind students that they are fact finders on a research mission. Some questions to ask students include:

- What have you learned about the packages?
- Are your findings important to you?
- Do class discoveries support individual data?
- What conclusions can be drawn?
- What discoveries were made?
- What should be communicated to the company?

BUSINESS LETTER

Review the business letter format with students before they begin the letter writing process. This portion of the task may be integrated into the language arts classroom and completed during that time.

RUBRIC

Rubrics are to be discussed at the same time the task explanation is distributed. Students should have copies of both available to them throughout the duration of the task. The rubric used for this task is a 4-point weighted rubric (see Figure 5.9). The layout of this rubric is different than others within the mathematics applications sections of previous chapters. The rubric is set up vertically, and levels of performance are listed beneath each other. The highest level of performance for each criterion is listed at the top of the section. Share all of the 4-point descriptors with students and point out the weights accompanying each section of the rubric.

Figure 5.9

When evaluating student performance, choose the descriptor for each criterion that best describes the product or performance. Each descriptor has a point value, and each section has a numerical weight. To calculate the value for each category, multiply the point value earned by the weight. When evaluation is complete, add all individual calculations together to obtain the total rubric score.

EXPANDING THE TASK

Graphing the results extends the performance task. Students can create a bar graph to record their data. A separate bar for each candy color will assist students in the comparisons they make. Creating a class or cooperative group multiple line graph also makes an interesting visual.

SIMPLIFYING THE TASK

The performance task can be simplified for younger students. To simplify, give every student the same number of candies; 25 works well. If there are more than 25 in the package, students are usually happy to eat a few. If there are fewer, hand out extras so each student has a total of 25. Students can concentrate on creating fractions representative of each color. Fractions can be compared throughout the class because the denominators will be the same. Decimals and fractions can be calculated as a class project. Calculators can help simplify this process.

CHECKUP

The assessment provided in the checkup (see Figure 5.10) is a traditional form of a teacher-made assessment. It can be used before or after the task. An answer key for the assessment is provided in Figure 5.11. Prior to the task, use the checkup to determine the current knowledge level of students. Then make instructional decisions regarding student readiness for the task. If used after completing the task, student performance will demonstrate the students' depth of understanding.

When tasks are completed, displaying student work adds to students' sense of accomplishment. Encourage students to explain their projects and findings to other students. This will increase their level of understanding.

Figure 5.10

Figure 5.11

— ∞ —

In Summary

When students are interested in their work, they learn more and retain information longer. The task provided in this chapter will interest students and give them opportunities to practice skills and explain thinking. The task assists students in seeing the relationships among fractions, decimals, and percents.

The weighted rubric provides clear expectations and gives students a target. In this task, calculating fractions, decimals, and percents and being able to explain procedure are worth more than some of the other areas of the task; therefore, a weighted rubric is used. Teachers can experiment with point values when they create rubrics that require varied point values.

Discoveries in Rainbow Candy Land

Task Explanation and Suggested Procedures

Task:

The Rainbow Candy Corporation has uncovered possible inconsistencies within their fun size packages of colored candies. Customers have been voicing their opinions about varying amounts of colors between packages. The research department is requesting your help. They need you to determine if the claims are accurate. They would also like a report of your findings.

Suggested Procedures:

1. Find out how many candies there are of each color. Write each number as a fraction of the total and as a decimal and a percent.

2. Organize the information on an easy-to-understand chart.

3. Explain how you arrived at your mathematical answers.

4. Share your findings with the class. Discuss class discoveries.

5. Write a letter to the Rainbow Candy Corporation sharing class findings. Include observations and recommendations.

Figure 5.4

Discoveries in Rainbow Candy Land

Data Collection Chart

Use this graphic organizer to record the candy color information and the fractions, decimals, and percents.

Procedures:

1. In the first column, write the names of all the colors found in your package of candy.
2. In the second column, write the number of candies you have of each color.
3. In the third column, write the fraction for each color. The numerator is the number of candy in the specific color, the denominator is the total number of candies in the package.
4. In the fourth column, record the decimals that correspond to each fraction. To calculate the decimal, divide the numerator of each fraction by its denominator.
5. In the last column, write each number as a percent of the total. To change the decimal to a percent, multiply by 100 (or move the decimal two places to the right).

Colors	Number of Candies per Color	Number as Fraction	Number as Decimal	Number as Percent
Totals				

Figure 5.5

Discoveries in Rainbow Candy Land

Data Collection Chart – Sample Key

Use this graphic organizer to record the candy color information, the fractions, decimals, and percents.

Procedures:
1. In the first column, write the names of all the colors found in your package of candy.
2. In the second column, write the number of candies you have of each color.
3. In the third column, write the fraction for each color. The numerator is the number of candy in the specific color, the denominator is the total number of candies in the package.
4. In the fourth column, record the decimals that correspond to each fraction. To calculate the decimal, divide the numerator of each fraction by its denominator.
5. In the last column, write each number as a percent of the total. To change the decimal to a percent, multiply by 100 (or move the decimal two places to the right).

Colors	Number of Candies per Color	Number as Fraction	Number as Decimal	Number as Percent
orange	5	5/25 = 1/5	0.2	20%
green	6	6/25	0.24	24%
blue	7	7/25	0.28	28%
red	2	2/25	0.08	8%
yellow	5	5/25 = 1/5	0.2	20%
Totals	25	25/25	1.00	100%

Figure 5.6

Discoveries in Rainbow Candy Land
Explanations and Examples

Answer questions in complete sentences.

How did you create the fractions on your chart?

How did you change the fractions into decimals? Include an example.

How did you change the decimals to percents? Include an example.

What discoveries did you make about your data?

Figure 5.7

SkyLight Professional Development

Discoveries in Rainbow Candy Land
Explanations and Examples – Sample Answers

Answer questions in complete sentences.

How did you create the fractions on your chart?

I put the number from the color over the total number candies.

How did you change the fractions into decimals? Include an example.

I divided the numerator by the denominator.
2/25 would be 2 ÷ 25.

How did you change the decimals to percents? Include an example.

I multiplied the decimal by 100.
.08 x 100 = 8%

What discoveries did you make about your data?

I found out that my data was different from what other kids found in their packages.

Figure 5.8

Discoveries in Rainbow Candy Land

Rubric

Instructions: Circle or highlight the appropriate point values. Multiply each by the weight of the category. Add all points together.

Performance		Value x Weight = Total	
Chart	Chart is complete, neat, and easy to read	4	
	Chart is neat and easy to read, 1 item missing	3	x 2 = _____
	Chart is neat and easy to read, 2 items missing	2	
	Chart is messy or 3 .or more items are missing	1	
Fractions	All fractions are present and accurate	4	
	1 fraction is incorrect or not present	3	x 5 = _____
	2 fractions are incorrect or not present	2	
	3 or more fractions are incorrect or not present	1	
Decimals	All decimals are present and accurate	4	
	1 decimal is incorrect or not present	3	x 5 = _____
	2 decimals are incorrect or not present	2	
	3 or more decimals are incorrect or not present	1	
Percents	All percents are present and accurate	4	
	1 percent is incorrect or not present	3	x 5 = _____
	2 percents are incorrect or not present	2	
	3 or more percents are incorrect	1	
Explanations	Explanations present for fractions, decimals, and percents Well-written and easy to understand Examples are included Grammar and spelling are perfect	4	
	Explanations present for fractions, decimals, and percents Well written and easy to understand Grammar and spelling are perfect	3	
	Explanations present for fractions, decimals, and percents confusing OR 1–3 grammar and spelling errors	2	x 10 = _____
	Explanations have portions missing OR confusing OR 4 or more grammar and spelling errors	1	
Letter	Form includes correct heading, inside address, greeting, body, closing, and signature Well written, neat, and easy to understand All punctuation, grammar, and spelling is accurate	4	
	Form includes correct heading, inside address, greeting, body, closing, and signature Well written, neat, and easy to understand 1–2 errors in punctuation, grammar, or spelling	3	x 3 = _____
	Form includes correct heading, inside address, greeting, body, closing, and signature Well written, neat, and easy to understand 3–4 errors in punctuation, grammar, or spelling	2	
	Proper form not used OR 5 or more errors in punctuation, grammar, or spelling	1	

Evaluator: _____   Points Possible = 120   Points Earned = _____

Figure 5.9

Discoveries in Rainbow Candy Land

Fractions, Decimals, and Percents Checkup   page 1

Name: _____   Points earned: _____/40   Grade: _____

Circle the letter of the correct answer. (1 point each)

1. 1/4 =
    a) 0.14   b) 0.25   c) 0.4   d) 2.5

2. 3/5 =
    a) 1.67   b) 0.35   c) 0.6   d) 3.5

3. 2³/₄ =
    a) 2.75   b) 2.34   c) 2.133   d) 27.5

4. 5³/₈ =
    a) 53.75   b) 5.375   c) 537.5   d) 5.267

5. 5.67 =
    a) 0.0567%   b) 0.567%   c) 56.7%   d) 567%

6. 0.45 =
    a) 45%   b) 4.5%   c) 0.0045%   d) 0.045%

7. 62% =
    a) 6.2   b) 0.62   c) 6200   d) 620.0

8. 358% =
    a) 35.8   b) 3.58   c) 358   d) 3580

9. 3/12 =
    a) 312%   b) 4%   c) 25%   d) 40%

10. 3/10 =
    a) 30%   b) 310%   c) 33.3%   d) 0.3%

Fill in the blank with the correct response. (3 points each)

11. The top number of a fraction is called a _____.

12. The bottom number of a fraction is called a _____.

13. The % sign represents the word _____.

14. When changing a decimal to a percent, the decimal point moves to the _____.

Write a short answer. (3 points each)
15. How do you change a fraction to a decimal? _____

_____

_____

_____

_____

Figure 5.10

16. Mrs. Etser spends about $3.00 out of every $8.00 of her money on food for her family. What percent of money does she spend on food? Explain your answer.

_____

_____

17. 85% of Mr. Ducken's class wore red during Red Ribbon Week. 7 out of every 8 of Mrs. Crosbert's students wore red. Which class had the higher percentage of students wearing red? Explain your answer.

_____

_____

_____

18. Mrs. Mortler, the principal, said that if the student body could raise 75% of the cost of a new playground, the school could afford the rest. The playground cost is $30,000. The students raised $23,000. Was that enough money to get the playground? Explain your answer.

_____

_____

_____

19. Mrs. Klima, the manager of a local toy store, did a study to see how many of her customers were children. She found that from 10:00 a.m. until 2:00 p.m. 6 out of every 8 customers were children. Between the hours of 2:00 p.m. and 6:00 p.m., 9 out of every 15 customers were children. During which hours are there a higher percent of children in the store? What are the percents?

_____

_____

_____

20. Mrs. Brecker plants a variety of flowers in her garden. She is interested in keeping track of the percent of each type of flower she plants this year. Her garden consists of 17 geraniums, 13 begonias, 9 mums, and 11 zinnias. What percent of her garden is made up of each type of flower?

_____

_____

_____

Figure 5.10 continued

Discoveries in Rainbow Candy Land

Fractions, Decimals, and Percents Checkup – Key   page 1

Name: _____   Points earned: _____ /50   Grade: _____

Circle the letter of the correct answer. (1 point each)

1. 1/4 =
   a) 0.14   (b) 0.25)   c) 0.4   d) 2.5

2. 3/5 =
   a) 1.67   b) 0.35   (c) 0.6)   d) 3.5

3. $2^3/_4$ =
   (a) 2.75)   b) 2.34   c) 2.133   d) 27.5

4. $5^3/_8$ =
   a) 53.75   (b) 5.375)   c) 537.5   d) 5.267

5. 5.67 =
   a) 0.0567%   b) 0.567%   c) 56.7%   (d) 567%)

6. 0.45 =
   (a) 45%)   b) 4.5%   c) 0.0045%   d) 0.045%

7. 62% =
   a) 6.2   (b) 0.62)   c) 6200   d) 620.0

8. 358% =
   a) 35.8   (b) 3.58)   c) 358   d) 3580

9. 3/12 =
   a) 312%   b) 4%   (c) 25%)   d) 40%

10. 3/10 =
    (a) 30%)   b) 310%   c) 33.3%   d) 0.3%

Fill in the blank with the correct response. (3 points each)

11. The top number of a fraction is called a _____numerator_____.

12. The bottom number of a fraction is called a _____denominator_____.

13. The % sign represents the word __percent_____.

14. When changing a decimal to a percent, the decimal point moves to the ___right_____.

Write a short answer. (3 points)

15. How do you change a fraction to a decimal? __Divide the numerator by the denominator.__

_____

_____

_____

Figure 5.11

Fractions, Decimals, and Percents Checkup – Key   page 2

16. Mrs. Etser spends about $3.00 out of every $8.00 of her money on food for her family. What percent of money does she spend on food? Explain your answer.

    3/8 of her money is equal to 37.5%. That means she spends 37.5% of her money on food.

17. 85% of Mr. Ducken's class wore red during Red Ribbon Week. 7 out of every 8 of Mrs. Crosbert's students wore red. Which class had the higher percentage of students wearing red? Explain your answer.

    7 out of 8 students is equal to 87.5% so Mrs. Crosbert had more students wearing red.

18. Mrs. Mortler, the principal, said that if the student body could raise 75% of the cost of a new playground, the school could afford the rest. The playground cost is $30,000. The students raised $23,000. Was that enough money to get the playground? Explain your answer.

    23000/30000 is equal to about 77% so the students did raise enough money.

19. Mrs. Klima, the manager of a local toy store, did a study to see how many of her customers were children. She found that from 10:00 a.m. until 2:00 p.m. 6 out of every 8 customers were children. Between the hours of 2:00 p.m. and 6:00 p.m., 9 out of every 15 customers were children. During which hours are there a higher percent of children in the store? What are the percents?

    More children were in the store between 10:00 and 2:00. 75% were children.

    Between 2:00 and 6:00 only 60% were children.

20. Mrs. Brecker plants a variety of flowers in her garden. She is interested in keeping track of the percent of each type of flower she plants this year. Her garden consists of 17 geraniums, 13 begonias, 9 mums, and 11 zinnias. What percent of her garden is made up of each type of flower?

    Geraniums = 34%   Begonias = 26%

    Mums = 18%   Zinnias = 22%

Figure 5.11 continued

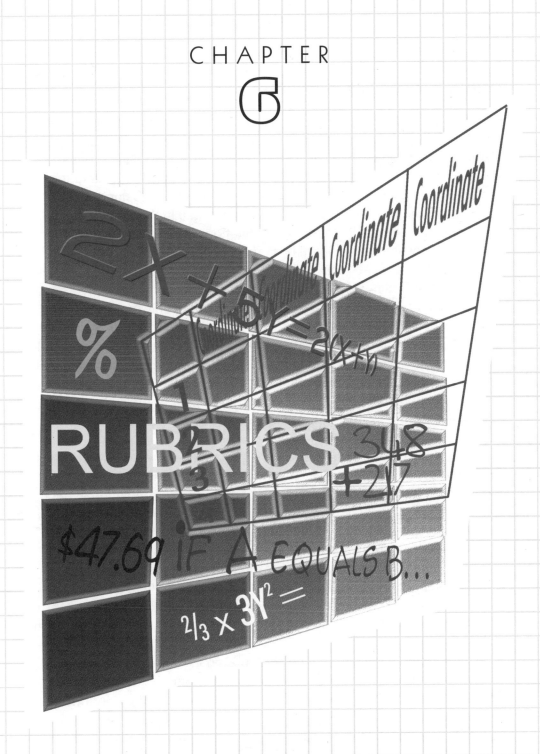

Student-Created
Rubrics

Using Student-Created Rubrics

Students, as well as everyone else, appreciate having input into things that affect their lives. When students are being evaluated on a product or performance, they may feel that it is crucial that their input is a part of the process. When this input occurs, students gain a deeper understanding of the task they are performing. They not only come to understand what is expected of them, but they begin to feel ownership in the process because they were able to contribute to the expectations.

In order for students to learn best, mathematics must be made meaningful to them, and they must be shown the purpose of their studies in a real-world setting. Therefore, performance tasks and problems should be based on mathematics applications—tasks that apply mathematics to a nontextbook setting and actively involve the student. Such mathematics applications must be evaluated with task-specific rubrics that allow students to solve problems they might find in everyday life. For example, using mathematics to figure out a monthly budget or to determine the best deal on a car loan are both examples of real-world mathematics applications. With some initial teacher direction, students can become experts at helping to create rubrics.

To develop rubrics, students require guidance for the performance task focus and essential knowledge. Teachers can help students discern task focus by asking them what is expected of them upon completion, what they should know and be able to do, and what the evidence will look like. Students are often adept at understanding the purpose of a task and can normally list the criteria fairly well. However, if students miss something crucial to the understanding, the teacher should be prepared to ask students to add that component. With practice, students will be able to pinpoint important criteria and describe what a high level of performance looks like for those criteria, as well as provide insight into mathematical quality performance descriptors.

There are many benefits when students aid in rubric development. Developing rubrics helps students clearly understand the task, the expectations, and the evaluation process. Students take pride in their performance and ownership in the entire process (Ainsworth and Christinson 1998). Students have much to contribute to a rubric and are more motivated to produce high-quality work when they are involved in the process, and teachers often find that the quality of the students' products often increases noticeably when they use student-generated rubrics (Danielson 1997).

To fully support student-created rubrics, teachers must recognize how important it is for students to take responsibility for their learning. It is crucial that students understand the reasons material is being presented to them as well as the part they play in the development of that knowledge. Through the rubric development process, students begin to understand the importance of assessment criteria. They gain a deeper comprehension into the purpose and the depth of their own understanding. Providing students with the opportunity to pinpoint the knowledge essential to understanding a concept gives them experience with thinking critically about what is important in the demonstration of knowledge. As a result, they become aware of what they need to know and at what level they need to perform for a successful experience.

In addition, when students contribute to a rubric, they typically find themselves more accountable to the standards. They internalize the standards and gain an in-depth comprehension of concepts. As a result of the discussion, students understand the role standards play in rubric development and, thus, project success. The rubric has the capability of providing focus and inspiring motivation (Rose 1999); in this way, the rubric not only acts as an assessment tool for students, but becomes a learning tool as well.

The Process

A teacher can start the student rubric development process by focusing on the task standards. The task standards link is crucial when developing and evaluating a real-life application. The teacher needs to make sure that successful completion of the task shows that students have grasped the knowledge essential to the standards. When the teacher is certain that the task relates to the standards and the details of the performance have been outlined, he or she should share the task with the students. The teacher must clearly explain the task to help students create the evaluation rubric. To provide valuable input, students need to understand the task and its intended purpose. The teacher can also discuss the standards and benchmarks with students to help them develop criteria for the rubric.

Next, the teacher should distribute a blank rubric to the students (see Figure 6.1) and request their suggestions for what is important for successful completion of the task. The think-write-pair-share strategy is a good tool to use during this time (see Figure 6.2). The teacher can allow students two minutes of brainstorming time to generate some appropriate criteria, ask students to spend another one or two minutes writing the criteria on the back of their blank rubric, and then give them two minutes to share their criteria with a partner and add more ideas to their own lists.

The next step is to create a list of criteria with the class. Teachers can solicit responses from as many pairs as necessary until all ideas have been shared and the list has been generated. At this point, any essential criteria that are not currently on the list should be added by prompting students into seeing the importance of the additions. Asking students questions such as, Do you think we might add . . . ?, How will we evaluate . . . ?, or Have we covered this standard?, will help generate additional responses.

At this point, the list needs to be grouped, combined, and pared down. Similar criteria should be grouped, and criteria that are alike should be

Student-Generated Rubric

Task: _____

Criteria	Levels of Quality — Descriptors			
	1 ◯	2 ☺	3 ☺	4 ☺

Figure 6.1

Think-Write-Pair-Share

THINK—Spend 2 minutes thinking of criteria or evidence that is crucial to the completion of the task.

WRITE—Spend 1–2 minutes writing a list of points from the Think Step.

PAIR—Quickly choose a partner.

SHARE—Spend 2 minutes sharing your list with your partner. Add your partners' ideas to your list.

Figure 6.2

combined. The teachers should discuss with students any criteria that might not apply or would not be possible to evaluate, and eliminate them. It is important that the final criteria accurately measure the performance. Five to ten criteria are reasonable.

Students can place the criteria list on their rubrics and begin developing descriptors in cooperative groups or as an entire class. Students should concentrate on a level 4 performance first. The teacher should stress to students that descriptors must be very specific, and that students should ask themselves what an exemplary level of accomplishment looks like and describe that. The teacher can encourage students to be realistic but to set high expectations. If the task is one that has been completed by a previous group of students, the teacher can show examples of the finished performances to help students visualize and describe top levels of quality. When this process is used regularly, students become experts in the development process.

Student input can end at this point. The impact of the rubric on student performance results from students taking ownership of the criteria and the descriptors at the highest level of quality. To save time, the teacher can complete levels 1 through 3 without further student input and present them to the class.

Teachers can then create the master rubric using student-generated criteria and descriptors for level 4. This can be done by collecting the descriptors and summarizing them when making the final rubric. After the rubric is complete, the teacher should discuss all the criteria and descriptors with students and distribute the final rubric before they begin the task.

A summary of these steps is provided in Figure 6.3.

Steps for Creating Student-Generated Rubrics

1. The teacher develops a performance task based on standards and benchmarks.

2. The teacher describes the performance task and its purpose to students.

3. Students develop evaluation criteria.

4. Students create descriptors for level 4.

5. The teacher creates descriptors for levels 1-3.

6. The teacher completes and distributes the rubric.

Figure 6.3

Evaluating student understanding and performance can be an enlightening experience for both students and teachers when students take an active part in the assessment process. Student-created rubrics result in products that exhibit increased levels of quality and students who demonstrate a new level of pride in their accomplishments.

— ∞ —

RUBRIC/MATHEMATICS APPLICATION

I'm Not Just Average!

In the following rubric/mathematics application, students calculate mean, median, mode, and range. The rubric used within this application was developed with students. Teachers can use this rubric or create a rubric with their students. The task overview (see Figure 6.4) outlines the basic information about the task.

PERFORMANCE TASK EXPLANATION

Many students are involved in sports both within and outside of school. Sports statistics are kept for every facet of professional athletics, and many are recorded for recreational programs as well. Students are aware of batting averages, free throw percentages, percentage of pass completions, average number of assists per game, bowling averages, average number of yards per drive, and hundreds more statistics for every sport imaginable. One of the many purposes of this task is to have students calculate statistics. Another is to have students use statistical information to form an opinion about a team and its season. This task takes approximately four 45-minute class periods.

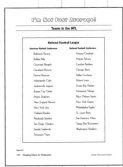

Figure 6.5

Any sport could be the subject of this task. Football was chosen because there are fewer games per season than the majority of other professional sports, which makes calculations easier for students. Some students may need assistance picking a team to use for the task. The teams in the NFL are listed in Figure 6.5, and this information can be copied and passed out to students.

The team's previous season's scores and opponents will be listed on the team's Web site. This information also can be researched through the National Football League at <www.nfl.com>. Students can print out the information or copy it onto their record chart. Figure 6.6 outlines the problem and procedures for students.

Figure 6.6

Following the gathering of data using the data collection chart (see Figure 6.7), students can create a graphic organizer to record the mean, median, mode, and range for the scores the team achieved. The graphic organizer included in Figure 6.8 could also be used for this purpose. Students should also

Figure 6.7   **Figure 6.8**

find the mean, median, mode, and range of the combined opponents' scores.

· UNIT OVERVIEW ·
I'm Not Just Average!

STANDARDS   Numbers and Operations, Data Analysis and Probability, Problem Solving, Communication, Connections

MATHEMATICS CONCEPTS   Calculating mean, median, mode, and range

GRADE LEVELS   4 through 9

RELATED CURRICULAR AREAS   Language Arts—Writing an explanation; Technology—Using the Internet

MATERIALS NEEDED   Computer with Internet access

TASK   The National Football League (NFL) is experiencing a glitch in its new statistical software. Comparisons need to be made between teams and the previous season's scores, but the computers have malfunctioned. Without this information, record books cannot be filled out. The NFL needs your help in finding the statistics necessary to make the comparisons.

SUGGESTED STUDENT PROCEDURES

1. Choose your favorite NFL team. Using the Internet, find the final scores from all the previous season's games. Try the team's Web site or go to <www.nfl.com>.
2. Create a chart to record all scores in chronological order from the first to the last game. Include the opponents' team names on the chart.
3. Find the mean, median, mode, and range of all the scores achieved by your team.
4. Find the mean, median, mode, and range of the combined opponents' scores.
5. Write a paragraph describing your team's season. Include comparisons among the mean, median, and mode. Express your opinions.
6. Organize the information into a booklet. Include explanations of the process used to find the mean, median, mode, and range.

TEACHER RESOURCES

Teams in the NFL page
Task Explanation and Suggested Procedure page
Data Collection Chart
Explanations and Statistics Organizer

Checklist
Rubric
Measure of Central Tendency Checkup and Key

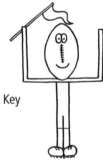

INTERNET RESOURCES

All Math: Offers tools and activities for students, including a mathematics glossary, metric conversion tools, flash cards, games, and links to other mathematics sites. <http://www.allmath.com>

Mudd Math Fun Facts: Features fun facts for areas of mathematics study from geometry to calculus for teachers to use in classroom discussion. <http://www.math.hmc.edu/funfacts>

Algebra Help: Helps students with algebra questions by offering lesson summaries, a calculator that takes students through the steps of solving the problem, and interactive worksheets. <http://www.algebrahelp.com>

Figure 6.4

118

SkyLight Professional Development

If the teacher's goal for this assignment includes reviewing whole number and decimal operations, students may be asked to show all calculations. If finding statistical information is the only goal, students can use calculators.

Students should describe the method used to find the mean, median, mode, and range. The numbers and equations should be included within their explanations. When calculations are complete, students can place results in the proper location on the graphic organizer.

REFLECTIONS

Once students have gathered their statistics, they need to take time to analyze the results. Probing questions might help students look at data more deeply. Some questions teachers can ask include:

- Which average makes your team look the best: mean, median, or mode?
- Which average would typically be reported?
- What can you conclude about the season by looking at the range?
- Could the mean of the choice team versus the mean of the opponent's team indicate a winning or losing season?
- Why do teams keep statistics?

After group discussion and comparison of results, students should write a personal reaction to their team's season. The statistical information they discover should be used within their reflections.

CHECKLIST

The checklist in Figure 6.9 provides a simple reminder for students and can be posted in the room or distributed the day before the task is to be completed. By comparing what they have completed to the task components listed in the checklist, students will become aware of the steps needed to complete the performance task.

Figure 6.9

RUBRIC

The left side of this student-created rubric (see Figure 6.10) lists the components the students deemed to be important. The 3-point column describes the level of quality that students felt would illustrate a quality product. Although this is a 4-column rubric, its top value is only 3 points because students wanted the first column to be worth zero. The students made this decision because they felt that if a portion of the project was missing, its creator should not be rewarded by accumulating points for work not attempted. For this task, students helped develop criteria for levels 1-3 in addition to criteria for the level 4 performance, because they had experience in rubric development and wanted to extend their input into the rubric development process.

Figure 6.10

The day the project is due, students should peer-evaluate the projects by completing the rubric. This task should be taken seriously since the goal is for students to help each other see the strengths and weaknesses of their projects. Students should then be allowed to improve their performances before the final grade is given. Extending the due date by a day or two increases the level of quality exhibited in the products. The goal of any performance is to have students achieve at the highest level possible. If extending a deadline by a short amount of time does that, the extension is well worth it.

EXPANDING THE TASK

The performance task can be expanded by assigning different teams to students, so that each student is responsible for a different team's statistics. Instead of writing reflections, students can write newspaper articles or editorials describing the team's season. These works, combined with season results and statistics, can be compiled and placed in an NFL informational booklet created by the class. Each chapter can highlight a different team, and students can create a chapter cover with team logos and names of players. They can even research the history of the team and insert additional information into their chapters. The completed booklet can be copied and distributed to school libraries within the district. Parents might also appreciate a copy.

SIMPLIFYING THE TASK

Students can be allowed to use calculators to complete all mathematical operations. This gives them the opportunity to work with statistics without being restricted by their ability to calculate.

To simplify the task for younger students, the teacher can concentrate on the mean and eliminate the median and the mode. The mean is the most common statistical average and students will benefit from understanding its use.

If teachers want to leave the task as is, but still simplify it, cooperative groups are a good option. Group members can work together to aid each other in comprehension and task completion.

CHECKUP

The Measures of Central Tendency assessment in Figure 6.11 is a combination of multiple choice, matching, and short answer questions. The assessment gives students several opportunities to illustrate their knowledge of mean, median, mode, and range. The assessment can be used as a follow-up

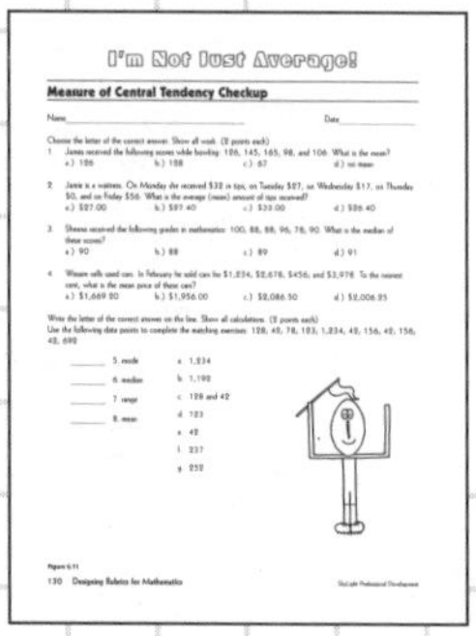

Figure 6.11

to the task or as an opportunity for practice before the task instead of a test. A key for the test is provided in Figure 6.12.

— ∞ —

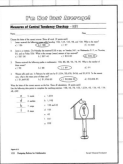

Figure 6.12

In Summary

Student-created rubrics are powerful tools, because getting students involved in the evaluation process motivates them to succeed. Students are more likely to understand expectations and strive to perform at their highest levels of ability when they take part in creating the evaluation tool. They are also more likely to see the evaluation tool as a fair measure of abilities when they are given a chance to provide their input. In this way, student-created rubrics drive student performance.

I'm Not Just Average!

National Football League

American Football Conference	National Football Conference
Baltimore Ravens	Arizona Cardinals
Buffalo Bills	Atlanta Falcons
Cincinnati Bengals	Carolina Panthers
Cleveland Browns	Chicago Bears
Denver Broncos	Dallas Cowboys
Indianapolis Colts	Detroit Lions
Jacksonville Jaguars	Green Bay Packers
Kansas City Chiefs	Minnesota Vikings
Miami Dolphins	New Orleans Saints
New England Patriots	New York Giants
New York Jets	Philadelphia Eagles
Oakland Raiders	St. Louis Rams
Pittsburgh Steelers	San Francisco 49ers
San Diego Chargers	Tampa Bay Buccaneers
Seattle Seahawks	Washington Redskins
Tennessee Titans	

Figure 6.5

I'm Not Just Average!

Task Explanation and Suggested Procedures

Task:

The National Football League (NFL) is experiencing a glitch in its new statistical software. Comparisons need to be made between teams and the previous season's scores, but the computers have malfunctioned. Without this information, record books cannot be filled out. The NFL needs your help in finding the statistics necessary to make the comparisons.

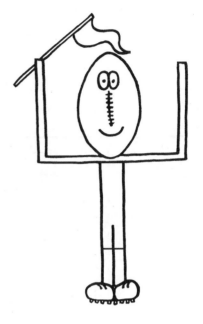

Suggested Procedures:

1. Choose your favorite NFL team. Using the Internet, find the final scores from all the previous season's games. Try the team's Web site or go to <www.nfl.com>.

2. Create a chart to record all scores in chronological order from the first to the last game. Include the opponents' team names on the chart.

3. Find the mean, median, mode, and range of all the scores achieved by your team.

4. Find the mean, median, mode, and range of the combined opponents' scores.

5. Write a paragraph describing your team's season. Include comparisons among the mean, median, and mode. Express your opinions.

6. Organize the information into a booklet. Include explanations of the process used to find the mean, median, mode, and range.

Figure 6.6

I'm Not Just Average!

Data Collection Chart

Team Name and Season Year

Game Number	My Team's Score	Opponent's Score	Opponent's Name
1			
2			
3			
4			
5			
6			
7			
8			
9			
10			
11			
12			
13			
14			
15			
16			

Figure 6.7

I'm Not Just Average!

Explanations and Statistics Organizer

Finding the Mean

Explanation:

Finding the Median

Explanation:

Finding the Mode

Explanation:

Finding the Range

Explanation:

Teams	Mean	Median	Mode	Range
Your Team's Scores				
Opponents' Combined Scores				

Figure 6.8

I'm Not Just Average!

Checklist

Do you have . . .	Yes	Not yet
A data chart of all previous season's scores for your team?		
An explanation of how to find the mean?		
The mean of your team and the opponents' combined mean?		
An explanation of how to find the median?		
The median of your team and the opponents' combined median?		
An explanation of how to find the mode?		
The mode of your team and the opponents' combined mode?		
An explanation of how to find the range?		
The range of your team and the opponents' combined range?		
A paragraph indicating your opinions comparing the season and the statistics you found?		
Correct spelling?		
A neat and attractive booklet?		
Your name on the booklet?		

Figure 6.9

I'm Not Just Average!

Rubric

Instructions: Highlight the area for each category that best describes the performance. Add points together to determine rubric score.

	0	1	2	3
Data Chart	Not present	Incomplete	Complete, lacks neatness	Complete, neat
Mean Your team	Not present	Mean or procedure inaccurate	Mean correct, procedure incomplete	Mean correct, procedure well illustrated
Opposing team	Not present	Mean or procedure inaccurate	Mean correct, procedure needs clarification	Mean correct, procedure well illustrated
Explanation	Not present or incorrect	Unclear	Correct with spelling errors	Well thought out, clear explanation
Median Your team	Not present	Median or procedure inaccurate	Median correct, procedure incomplete	Median correct, procedure well illustrated
Opposing team	Not present	Median or procedure inaccurate	Median correct, procedure needs clarification	Median correct, procedure well illustrated
Explanation	Not present or incorrect	Unclear	Correct with spelling errors	Well thought out, clear explanation
Mode Your team	Not present	Mode or procedure inaccurate	Mode correct, procedure incomplete	Mode correct, procedure well illustrated
Opposing team	Not present	Mode or procedure inaccurate	Mode correct, procedure needs clarification	Mode correct, procedure well illustrated
Explanation	Not present or incorrect	Unclear	Correct with spelling errors	Well thought out, clear explanation
Range Your team	Not present	Range or procedure inaccurate	Range correct, procedure incomplete	Range correct, procedure well illustrated
Opposing team	Not present	Range or procedure inaccurate	Range correct, procedure needs clarification	Range correct, procedure well illustrated
Explanation	Not present or incorrect	Unclear	Correct with spelling errors	Well thought out, well illustrated
Booklet	Not present or largely incomplete	Disorganized, information missing	Complete, organized	Complete, organized, attractive

Points possible=42   Points earned=

Figure 6.10

I'm Not Just Average!

Measure of Central Tendency Checkup   page 1

Name_____   Date_____

Choose the letter of the correct answer. Show all work. (2 points each)

1. James received the following scores while bowling: 126, 145, 165, 98, and 106. What is the mean?
    a.) 126   b.) 128   c.) 67   d.) no mean

2. Jamie is a waitress. On Monday she received $32 in tips, on Tuesday $27, on Wednesday $17, on Thursday $0, and on Friday $56. What is the average (mean) amount of tips received?
    a.) $27.00   b.) $27.40   c.) $33.00   d.) $26.40

3. Sheena received the following grades in mathematics: 100, 88, 88, 96, 78, 90. What is the median of these scores?
    a.) 90   b.) 88   c.) 89   d.) 91

4. Wassim sells used cars. In February he sold cars for $1,234, $2,678, $456, and $3,978. To the nearest cent, what is the mean price of these cars?
    a.) $1,669.20   b.) $1,956.00   c.) $2,086.50   d.) $2,006.25

Write the letter of the correct answer on the line. Show all calculations. (2 points each)
Use the following data points to complete the matching exercises: 128, 42, 78, 123, 1,234, 42, 156, 42, 156, 42, 692

_____ 5. mode   a. 1,234

_____ 6. median   b. 1,192

_____ 7. range   c. 128 and 42

_____ 8. mean   d. 123

                               e. 42

                               f. 248.63

                               g. 252

Figure 6.11

I'm Not Just Average!

Name_____   Date_____

Find answers for each problem. (20 points each)

9. The Green Bay Packers scored the following points in their first seven games: 27, 42, 0, 13, 21, 27, and 10. Find the mean, median, mode, and range.

_____

_____

10. Marissa got a new job. The first week she earned $130.25. The second week she earned $245.25. The third week she earned $238.75. This week she earned $312.75. Find the mean, median, mode, and range.

_____

_____

11. Andy wants his average bowling score to be no less than 120. The first game he bowled a 98. The second game he got 110. What is the lowest score he can get on the third game to have at least a 120 average?

_____

_____

12. Maria scored an average of 22 points in the first seven games of the basketball season. These are the scores for the first six games: 15, 18, 30, 12, 22, and 18. How many points did she score during the seventh game?

_____

_____

13. Rosie hopes to sell an average of at least $980 of merchandise each day in her store this week. On Sunday she took in $820, on Monday $675, on Tuesday $1,200, on Wednesday $1,000, on Thursday $726, and on Friday $1,300. What is the least amount of money she needs to take in on Saturday to reach her goal?

_____

_____

14. You received these five grade in mathematics: 88, 100, 88, 92, and 64. What is the mean, median, and mode of your grades?

_____

_____

Figure 6.11 continued

I'm Not Just Average!

Measures of Central Tendency Checkup – Key   page 1

Name_____   Date_____

Choose the letter of the correct answer. Show all work. (2 points each)

1. James received the following scores while bowling: 126, 145, 165, 98, and 106. What is the mean?

    a.) 126   (b.) 128)   c.) 67   d.) no mean

2. Jamie is a waitress. On Monday she received $32 in tips, on Tuesday $27, on Wednesday $17, on Thursday $0, and on Friday $56. What is the average (mean) amount of tips received?

    a.) $27.00   b.) $27.40   c.) $33.00   (d.) $26.40)

3. Sheena received the following grades in mathematics: 100, 88, 88, 96, 78, 90. What is the median of these scores?

    a.) 90   b.) 88   (c.) 89)   d.) 91

4. Wassim sells used cars. In February he sold cars for $1,234, $2,678, $456, and $3,978. To the nearest cent, what is the mean price of these cars?

    a.) $1,669.20   b.) $1,956.00   (c.) $2,086.50)   d.) $2,006.25

Write the letter of the correct answer on the line. Show all calculations. (2 points each)

Use the following data points to complete the matching exercises: 128, 42, 78, 123, 1,234, 42, 156, 42, 156, 42, 692

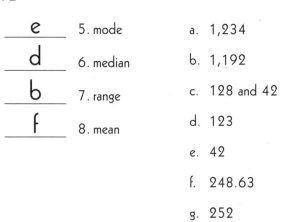

___e___	5. mode	a.	1,234
___d___	6. median	b.	1,192
___b___	7. range	c.	128 and 42
___f___	8. mean	d.	123
		e.	42
		f.	248.63
		g.	252

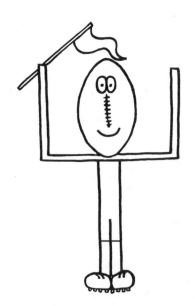

I'm Not Just Average!

Name_____   Date_____

Find answers for each problem. (20 points each)

9. The Green Bay Packers scored the following points in their first seven games: 27, 42, 0, 13, 21, 27, and 10. Find the mean, median, mode, and range.

   Mean = 20   Median = 21   Mode = 27   Range = 42

10. Marissa got a new job. The first week she earned $130.25. The second week she earned $245.25. The third week she earned $238.75. This week she earned $312.75 Find the mean, median, mode, and range.

   Mean = $231.75   Median = $242.00   Mode = none   Range = $182.50

11. Andy wants his average bowling score to be no less than 120. The first game he bowled a 98. The second game he got 110. What is the lowest score he can get on the third game to have at least a 120 average?

   152

12. Maria scored an average of 22 points in the first seven games of the basketball season. These are the scores for the first six games: 15, 18, 30, 12, 22, and 18. How many points did she score during the seventh game?

   39 points

13. Rosie hopes to sell an average of at least $980 of merchandise each day in her store this week. On Sunday she took in $820, on Monday $675, on Tuesday $1,200, on Wednesday $1,000, on Thursday $726 and on Friday $1,300. What is the least amount of money she needs to take in on Saturday to reach her goal?

   $1,139

14. You received these five grade in mathematics: 88, 100, 88, 92, and 64. What is the mean, median, and mode of your grades?

   Mean = 86.4   Median = 88   Mode = 88

Figure 6.12 continued

Teacher-Made Tests and the Rubric

Using Teacher-Made Tests

Teacher-made tests are important evaluation tools for student learning. Simply defined, a teacher-made test is an evaluation tool designed by a teacher for his or her students that can be used at any point during a unit of study. Often the most instructionally relevant tests are those created by a teacher for a specific group of students to emphasize information important to the concepts taught (Childs 1989).

This type of assessment helps to focus a teacher's instruction, because those concepts deemed most important to evaluate are also the concepts deemed most important to be learned. According to the NCTM (2000), assessment should result in informed teaching. The purpose of assessment is not only to monitor and evaluate, but also to enhance the learning process.

When used for formative purposes—to help guide student learning and increase student achievement—teacher-made tests can positively impact student knowledge. Using test results to evaluate what students know and need to learn is valuable, because the information gleaned from test results should guide classroom practices and instruction. The use of classroom data to modify instruction, coupled with the sharing of that data with students, can greatly impact student achievement (Jenkins 1997).

According to Black and Wiliam (1998), when teacher-made tests are used as a formative tool, the levels of overall achievement rise. The biggest impact is usually seen with low-achieving students, because these students typically benefit the most from guidance in discerning what they should focus on to increase learning and performance. Teaching and learning must be adjusted based on formative assessment results if evaluation is to influence achievement (Black and Wiliam 1998).

Many tests overemphasize memorization and skills and underemphasize knowledge and the useful performance of skills. Assessment results should display an accurate picture of what students know and how they are able to use that knowledge. Authentic simulations and problems—such as asking students to determine the length of a fence needed to surround the yard—can increase students' intellectual involvement in the test. When this occurs, the result is a more accurate picture of the students' ability to use their knowledge to create solutions to realistic situations (Wiggins 1992).

Creating a Teacher-Made Test

There are several factors to keep in mind when creating a test that assesses a students' knowledge and skills and that is beneficial for improving instruction.

Standards

The purpose of any unit of study and evaluation should be rooted in standards. Standards provide focus by defining what it is that students are expected to know, what they should be able to do, and how they are to apply that knowledge. Standards provide direction not only for teaching and learning, but also for assessment. A clear focus should be apparent at the onset of unit planning. Teachers need to consider questions such as:

- What knowledge should students have by the end of the unit of study?
- What knowledge is essential to the learning process?
- How should students be able to apply the knowledge?

Teacher-made tests should be developed around the answers to these three questions.

Tests should be created before the unit of study begins. This practice provides focus for developing classroom activities as it guides what should be taught and what should be learned. Various strategies can be planned to meet the needs of all learners. For example, a teacher may decide that cooperative grouping may assist in the learning process, or that graphic organizers would be useful in helping students organize thoughts, practices, and principles. Standards and goals should be shared with students prior to beginning the material so that students clearly understand expectations. The planning grid in Figure 7.1 can be used in the process of test development and to provide focus for the key content. Teachers can fill this out before beginning a unit to help clarify the goals of the teaching and learning.

Questions on a Teacher-Made Test

After standards and concepts have been defined and learning expectations are clear, the next step is to choose the types of questions to be used on the test. Questions should be varied in order to allow students to demonstrate their knowledge through various forms of questioning. Using different types of questions also allows teachers to get a clearer picture of student understanding. Some students are able to perform better on a specific type of question, and varying question types give students a better opportunity to excel at the task. Common types of questions include multiple choice, matching, completion, true-false, short answer, and essay. All types of questions do not need to be on every test, but all tests should include questions that allow students to apply their skills to problems that demonstrate understanding. When writing test questions, clarity is crucial. Students need to understand what they are expected to demonstrate when completing their response.

Essential Knowledge Planning Grid

Standards: _____

_____

Concepts: _____

_____

Students are expected to:

KNOW	DO	UNDERSTAND

Figure 7.1

SkyLight Professional Development

Figure 7.2 offers some tips teachers can use for constructing questions that elicit student understanding. As summarized in the figure, when developing true/false questions teachers should avoid words such as all, never, and always because these absolute words tend to confuse students. Students may know the material but get the answer wrong because of that confusion. Matching questions should be limited to between five and ten items so that the physical part of matching does not confuse the test taker. When multiple-choice questions are used, the main idea should be stated in the core of the sentence, because this focuses the test-taker on the core knowledge needed to answer the question. Multiple correct answers can be offered, because this challenges students to evaluate the choices at a greater depth. It also eliminates students simply guessing at which answer might be correct. When teachers create completion questions, they should avoid using passages directly lifted from their students' textbooks. Using textbook passages emphasizes memorization rather than higher-order thinking. Finally, with essay questions, it is important to define the criteria for evaluation so students clearly understand what they are being asked to explain. It is also beneficial to use higher-order thinking verbs—such as *evaluate, prediction, compare and contrast,* and *create*—rather than verbs that rely specifically on recall memory—such as *define, list,* or *name.*

Evaluating a Teacher-Made Test

After formulating test questions, a teacher can compare them to the Essential Knowledge Planning Grid (Figure 7.1) to be sure the questions address the goals of the teaching. Then, the teacher can ask him- or herself the following questions to be sure that the test includes all the information necessary to be a successful evaluation:

- Do the questions provide students with ample opportunity to demonstrate their grasp of the knowledge essential to key concepts?
- Does the successful completion of the assessment provide true evidence of understanding?
- At what level will students need to perform in order for the outcome to be deemed a success?
- What plans will be implemented for students who are unable to demonstrate a successful level of performance?
- What strategies will be employed to assist students in gaining a deeper understanding of concepts crucial to their success?

Once the teacher has answered these questions, he or she can use the Test Construction Rubric (see Figure 7.3) to further evaluate the test. The criteria listed were gathered from several sources, including educational Web sites, educational books, and educators themselves, and have been

---

Tips for Constructing Test Questions

True-False Questions
- Avoid absolute words like <u>all</u>, <u>never</u>, and <u>always</u>.
- Make sure items are clearly true or false rather than ambiguous.
- Limit true-false questions to ten.
- Consider asking students to make false questions true to encourage higher-order thinking.

Matching Questions
- Limit list to between five and ten items.
- Use homogeneous lists (e.g., do not mix names with dates).
- Give clear instructions.
- Give more choices than there are questions.

Multiple-Choice Questions
- State main idea in the core or stem of the question.
- Use reasonable incorrect choices. (Avoid ridiculous choices.)
- Make options the same length (nothing very long or very short).
- Include multiple correct answers (e.g., a and b, all of the above).

Completion Questions
- Structure for a brief specific answer for each item.
- Avoid passages lifted directly from text (doing so emphasizes memorization).
- Use blanks of equal length.
- Avoid multiple blanks that sometimes make a sentence too confusing.

Essay Questions
- Avoid all-encompassing questions. ("Discuss . . ." and "Tell all you know . . ." are ambiguous).
- Define criteria for evaluation.
- Give point value.
- Use some higher-order thinking verbs—such as <u>evaluate</u>, <u>predict</u>, <u>compare and contrast</u>, and <u>create</u> rather than all recall verbs—such as <u>define</u>, <u>list</u>, and <u>name</u>.

Adapted from *The Mindful School: How to Assess Authentic Learning*, by Kay Burke. © 1999 IRI/SkyLight Training and Publishing, Inc. Reprinted by permission of SkyLight Professional Development, Arlington Heights, IL.

Figure 7.2

deemed important to the test construction, implementation, and evaluation process. Teachers can rate their test by comparing it to each of the various criteria.

Sharing Test Results

Timely constructive feedback is important to the formative assessment process so students are still close to the learning and so that teachers can address any confusion on the part of students while the learning is still fresh in the students' minds. Written comments that assist students with improv-

Test Construction Rubric Points to consider	Needs work	Some evidence	Definitely!
The test is linked directly to the standards and benchmarks.			
The test was created before teaching the unit.			
The language is appropriate to the task and age level of the students.			
There are clear written directions for each section of the test.			
The types of test questions are varied and illustrate what students know and can do, and the questions contain applications to demonstrate understanding.			
The level of questioning is varied, and questions are arranged from easy questions to those that are more complex.			
Point values are listed for each section of the test.			
Students are expected to show their calculations or methods for obtaining answers.			
Sufficient time is allotted for completion of the test.			
Plans for evaluating and using test results are outlined in advance.			

Needs Work Indicates that the expectation has not been met or is a weak illustration of that aspect of the test.

Some Evidence Indicates that the expectation has been met but needs expansion or extension to better meet criteria.

Definitely Indicates that every expectation has been met and is an exemplary example of the criteria.

Figure 7.3

ing their performance are beneficial. Such comments should be positive and nonjudgmental, and should state what the student has completed and what still needs to be done to fulfill the assessment goal. For example, "You have clearly explained what the word *mean* refers to; now can you provide an example showing how to calculate the mean?" is more supportive than "You didn't give an example." Class discussions or a feedback session can be held when common misunderstandings arise among students. Students can provide insight into their thinking and the teacher can eliminate misconceptions and strengthen understandings.

According to the United States Department of Education (1993), sharing test results with students is an important part of the test taking process. Students need to understand their strengths and evaluate their weaknesses. Students also must understand errors and be given the opportunity to ask questions and clarify misconceptions.

— ∞ —

RUBRIC/MATHEMATICS APPLICATION

Finding LCM and GCF

This rubric/mathematics application covers the concepts of prime factorization, least common multiple (LCM), and greatest common factor (GCF). These concepts are foundational pieces that provide connections to understanding several mathematical operations. During the application, students will illustrate methods used to find LCM and GCF.

A teacher-made test is included with the chapter. The test can be used for formative or summative purposes. Using it in conjunction with the mathematics application helps students better understand the related mathematics concepts and ways that they apply the concepts to real-world situations.

PERFORMANCE TASK EXPLANATION

People often learn best by doing, and they are able to increase their understanding when they explain something to others. In this task, students are asked to explain

Figure 7.5

two methods of finding LCM and GCF to others. Their explanation includes illustrations of both methods and an example of a real-world application of the concept. An overview is provided in Figure 7.4, and a task explanation and suggested procedures are provided in Figure 7.5. Students will need to be introduced to both methods and be given the opportunity to do some practice before the task begins. Upon completing the task, students should be prepared to discuss which method they prefer and give justification for their answer. This application takes one or two 45-minute class periods.

The task could look like the examples in Figure 7.6. Students should be given the opportunity to be creative, however.

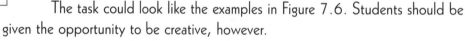

A=6xh

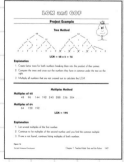

Figure 7.6

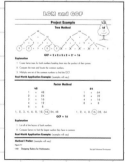

Figure 7.6, continued

▪ UNIT OVERVIEW ▪
Finding LCM and GCF

STANDARDS   Numbers and Operations, Problem Solving, Communication, Connections

MATHEMATICS CONCEPTS   Prime factorization, Least Common Multiple, Greatest Common Factor

GRADE LEVELS   3 through 9

RELATED CURRICULAR AREAS   Language Arts—Writing an explanation; Art—Creating a visual display

MATERIALS NEEDED   Construction paper, rulers

TASK   Ms. Ellers is a mathematics teacher who needs your help. Her students have been learning about Least Common Multiples (LCM) and Greatest Common Factors (GCF), but they get confused. She would like student input to decide the best method to teach and the best way to illustrate procedures.

SUGGESTED STUDENT PROCEDURES

1. Create a visual display illustrating:
   a. Two methods that can be used to find the Greatest Common Factor (GCF) of two numbers. First use the factor tree method, and then use the multiples listing method.
   b. Two methods that can be used to find the Least Common Multiple (LCM) for two numbers. First use the factor tree method, and then use the factor listing method.
2. Include a written explanation of each method. Include an example of a real-life application for both.
3. Explain which method you prefer and why.

TEACHER RESOURCES

Task Explanation and Suggested Procedure page
Project Example pages
Rubric
Prime Factorization/LCM/GCF Checkup pages and Keys

INTERNET RESOURCES

The Math Forum Internet Mathematics Library: Features links to mathematics resources, teaching strategies, and mathematics topics for various education levels. <http://www.forum.swarthmore.edu/library/>
AAA Math: A site containing lessons on many topics for teachers. <http://www.aaamath.com>
MathStories.com: Features over 4,000 mathematics word problems to help grade school students improve their problem-solving skills. <http://www.mathstories.com>

Figure 7.4

Figure 7.7

RUBRIC

Before beginning the task, students should be given a copy of the task (Figure 7.4) and the rubric (Figure 7.7). The rubric will guide students through the task. Being aware of criteria and expectations helps raise the level of performance.

EXPANDING THE TASK

When tasks are complete, students should be capable of teaching the concepts to other students. They should be very comfortable with prime factorization and finding GCF and LCM. At this point, the class could be paired up with another mathematics class at the same or at another grade level. Students could then illustrate and explain the processes to others, as well as discuss some real-life applications.

SIMPLIFYING THE TASK

To simplify, the task could be limited to one concept. Students could be expected to illustrate either prime factorization, finding the GCF, or finding the LCM.

CHECKUP (TEACHER-MADE TEST)

Students are expected to understand the concepts of prime factorization, GCF, and LCM. They manipulate numbers and solve problems that illustrate how well they are able to apply their skills.

The assessment in Figure 7.8 includes the important components of a teacher-made test. The types of questions are varied, each section indicates the point value that is available for each question, directions are given for each section of the test, and the level of questioning is varied.

Students are asked to show all work needed to complete their answers. This can be done on the assessment, or on a separate sheet of paper that is then attached to the test.

Test results should be shared with students as soon as possible. Teachers should explain any concepts that the test has shown to be unclear or confusing to students. If necessary, re-teaching should take place and students should be given additional opportunities to demonstrate their abilities.

A key to the assessment is provided in Figure 7.9.

— ∞ —

Figure 7.8

Figure 7.9

In Summary

Well-constructed teacher-made tests can guide the instruction process by highlighting the important concepts of a unit for teaching and learning purposes. Constructing a test based on standards before a unit of study begins helps maintain a clear focus throughout, and using test results to guide instruction increases the level of student achievement.

Finding LCM and GCF

Task Explanation and Suggested Procedures

Task:

Ms. Ellers is a mathematics teacher who needs your help. Her students have been learning about Least Common Multiples (LCM) and Greatest Common Factors (GCF), but they get confused. She would like student input to decide the best method to teach and the best way to illustrate procedures.

Suggested Procedures:

1. Create a visual display illustrating:

   a. Two methods that can be used to find the Greatest Common Factor (GCF) of two numbers. First use the factor tree method, and then use the multiples listing method.

   b. Two methods that can be used to find the Least Common Multiple (LCM) for two numbers. First use the factor tree method, and then use the factor listing method.

2. Include a written explanation of each method. Include an example of a real-life application for both.

3. Explain which method you prefer and why.

Figure 7.5

Finding LCM and GCF

LCM Tree Method

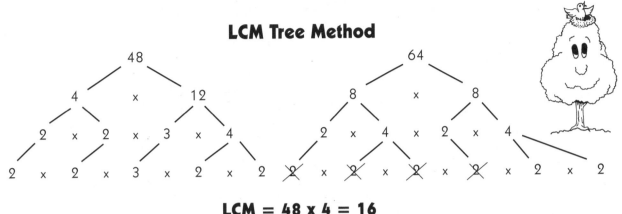

$$LCM = 48 \times 4 = 16$$

Explanation

1. Create factor trees for both numbers breaking them into the product of their primes.

2. Compare the trees and cross out the numbers they have in common under the tree on the right.

3. Multiply all numbers that are not crossed out to calculate the LCM.

Real-world Application Example: (examples will vary)

LCM Multiples Method

Multiples of 48
48   96   144   192   240   288   336   384 . . .

Multiples of 64
64   128   192 . . .

$$LCM = 192$$

Explanation

1. List several multiples of the first number.

2. Continue to list multiples of the second number until you find the common multiple.

3. If one is not found, continue listing multiples of both numbers.

Real-world Application Example (examples will vary)

Figure 7.6

Finding LCM and GCF

GCF Tree Method

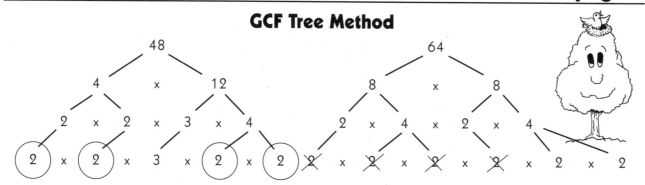

$$\text{GCF} = 2 \times 2 \times 2 \times 2 = 2^4 = 16$$

Explanation

1. Create factor trees for both numbers breaking them into the product of their primes.

2. Compare the trees and locate the common numbers.

3. Multiply one set of the common numbers to find the GCF.

Real-World Application Example: (examples will vary)

GCF Factor Method

48				**64**		
1	x	48		1	x	64
2	x	24		2	x	32
3	x	16		4	x	16
4	x	12		8	x	8
6	x	8				

1, 2, 3, 4, 6, 8, 12, (16,) 24, 48   1, 2, 4, 8, (16,) 32, 64

$$\text{GCF} = 16$$

Explanation

1. List all of the factors of both numbers.

2. Compare factors to find the largest number they have in common.

Real-World Application Example: (examples will vary)

Method I Prefer: (examples will vary)

Figure 7.6 continued

Finding LCM and GCF

Rubric

Least Common Multiple and Greatest Common Factor

Highlight the descriptor that most accurately describes the product. Add points to gain final score.

	0	**1**	**2**	**3**
LCM Tree Method Trees	Incomplete or not present	Inaccurate	Correct	Correct, neat, easy to read
LCM	Not present	Inaccurate	Correct	Correct, labeled with LCM= _____
Explanation	Not present or inaccurate	Difficult to understand	Clear and accurate	Clear, accurate, perfect spelling and punctuation
LCM Multiples Method Factor Lists	Not present or inaccurate	Accurate with 2 or more multiples missing	Accurate with 1 multiple missing	Accurate and complete
LCM	Not present	Inaccurate	Correct	Correct, labeled with LCM= _____
Explanation	Not present or inaccurate	Difficult to understand	Clear and accurate	Clear, accurate, perfect spelling and punctuation
GCF Tree Method Trees	Incomplete or not present	Inaccurate	Correct	Correct, neat, easy to read
GCF	Not present	Inaccurate	Correct	Correct, labeled with GCF= _____
Explanation	Not present or inaccurate	Difficult to understand	Clear and accurate	Clear, accurate, perfect spelling and punctuation
GCF Factor Method Factor Lists	Not present or inaccurate	Accurate with 2 or more factors missing	Accurate with 1 factor missing	Accurate and complete
GCF	Not present	Inaccurate	Correct	Correct, labeled with GCF= _____
Explanation	Not present or inaccurate	Difficult to understand	Clear and accurate	Clear, accurate, perfect spelling and punctuation
Neatness	Sloppy	Difficult to read without careful concentration	Neat	Neat and attractive

Evaluator:_____   Points possible =39   Points earned=_____

Figure 7.7

Finding LCM and GCF

Prime Factorization / LCM / GCF Checkup

Name _____   Date_____

Choose the letter of the correct answer. Show all work. (3 points each)

1. What is the prime factorization of 16?
   a.) 2 x 2x 2 x 2   b.) 4 x 4   c.) 2 x 8   d.) 8^2

2. What is the prime factorization of 64?
   a.) 8 x 8   b.) 2 x 32   c.) 2 x 2 x 2 x 2 x 2   d.) 2^6

3. What is the LCM of 16 and 64?
   a.) 16   b.) 8   c.) 64   d.) 128

4. What is the GCF of 16 and 64?
   a.) 4   b.) 8   c.) 16   d.) 64

Write the letter of the correct answer on the line. Show all work. (3 points each)

_____ 5. prime factorization of 120

_____ 6. prime factorization of 100

_____ 7. prime factorization of 144

_____ 8. LCM of 25 and 75

_____ 9. GCF of 60 and 80

_____ 10. LCM of 60 and 80

a. $2^2 \times 5^2$

b. 75

c. 20

d. 30

e. 122

f. $2^3 \times 3 \times 5$

g. $2 \times 3^2 \times 5$

h. 10^2

i. 240

j. $2^4 \times 3^2$

k. 150

Figure 7.8

SkyLight Professional Development

Finding LCM and GCF

Prime Factorization / LCM / GCF Checkup

Name _____   Date _____

Fill in the blanks with the word you feel would best complete the sentence. (10 points each)

11. $2^2 \times 3$ is the _____ (2 words) of the number 12.

12. 12 is the _____ (3 words) of 24 and 36.

13. 12 is the _____ (3 words) of 4 and 6.

Calculate and explain your answer. (20 points each)

14. Mr. Jackson has noticed that every fifth customer that enters his store buys bread. Every ninth person entering the store purchases milk. If Mr. Jackson has 120 customers enter his store today, how many will buy both milk and bread?

_____

_____

_____

_____

15. You are in charge of telling planes when to take off at Ames International Airport. The airport has decided that planes will take off on runway A every 15 minutes. Planes will take off on runway B every 10 minutes. Evaluate any problem this system might create. Discuss possible solutions.

Runway B

Runway A

_____

_____

_____

_____

Points possible = ___100___   Points earned = _____   Grade = _____

Figure 7.8 continued

Finding LCM and GCF

Prime Factorization / LCM / GCF Checkup – Key page 1

Name _____ Date _____

Choose the letter of the correct answer. Show all work. (3 points each)

1. What is the prime factorization of 16?
   (a.) 2 x 2x 2 x 2   b.) 4 x 4   c.) 2 x 8   d.) 8^2

2. What is the prime factorization of 64?
   a.) 8 x 8   b.) 2 x 32   c.) 2 x 2 x 2 x 2 x 2   (d.) 2^6)

3. What is the LCM of 16 and 64?
   a.) 16   b.) 8   (c.) 64)   d.) 128

4. What is the GCF of 16 and 64?
   a.) 4   b.) 8   (c.) 16)   d.) 64

Write the letter of the correct answer of the line. Show all work. (3 points each)

___f___   5. prime factorization of 120

___a___   6. prime factorization of 100

___j___   7. prime factorization of 144

___b___   8. LCM of 25 and 75

___c___   9. GCF of 60 and 80

___i___   10. LCM of 60 and 80

a. $2^2 \times 5^2$

b. 75

c. 20

d. 30

e. 122

f. $2^3 \times 3 \times 5$

g. $2 \times 3^2 \times 5$

h. 10^2

i. 240

j. $2^4 \times 3^2$

k. 150

Figure 7.9

SkyLight Professional Development

Finding LCM and GCF

Prime Factorization / LCM / GCF Checkup – Key   page 2

Name _____   Date_____

Fill in the blanks with the word you feel would best complete the sentence. (10 points each)

11. 2^2 x 3 is the ___prime factorization___ (2 words) of the number 12.

12. 12 is the ___greatest common factor___ (3 words) of 24 and 36.

13. 12 is the ___least common multiple___ (3 words) of 4 and 6.

Calculate and explain your answer. (20 points each).

14. Mr. Jackson has noticed that every fifth customer that enters his store buys bread. Every ninth person entering the store purchases milk. If Mr. Jackson has 120 customers enter his store today, how many will buy both milk and bread?

___There will be two customers that buy both bread and milk. The two common multiples___
___of 5 and 9 up to 120, are 45 and 90.___

15. You are in charge of telling planes when to take off at Ames International Airport. The airport has decided that planes will take off on runway A every 15 minutes. Planes will take off on runway B every ten minutes. Evaluate any problem this system might create. Discuss possible solutions.

___The planes will meet at the intersection of the runways every thirty minutes.___
___Solutions will vary.___

Points possible = ___100___   Points earned= _____   Grade= _____

Figure 7.9 continued

RUBRICS

Additional Math
Application Projects

Rubric/Mathematics Application Projects

The following are additional rubric/mathematics application projects that teachers can use in their classroom. Each project relates to NCTM standards, and contains a project overview that describes the project and the resources needed to conduct the project. The worksheets and rubrics needed to carry out the project in the classroom are also included.

▪ PROJECT 1 OVERVIEW ▪
Measurement and Statistics

STANDARDS   Measurement, Statistics (graphing), Communication, Problem Solving

MATHEMATICS CONCEPTS   Metric measurement of length, weight, and diameter, and graphing

GRADE LEVELS   2 through 7

MATERIALS NEEDED   Metric rulers and scale, string, graph paper, mini pumpkins

TASK   Determine who has the largest pumpkin.

SUGGESTED STUDENT PROCEDURES

1. Each individual or cooperative group will receive a pumpkin.

2. Discuss ways the largest pumpkin could be identified (weight, height, diameter). Choose a method for your group.

3. Using the proper measurement tool, find the measurement for each pumpkin in the group. (Diameter can be measured using a string and a ruler.)

4. Measurements can be made to the nearest centimeter and gram. Record all measurements on the chart.

5. Graph the data collected.

6. Complete the reflections page.

TEACHER RESOURCES

Task Explanation and Suggested Procedures page (Figure A1.2)

Reflections page (Figure A1.3)

Rubric (Figure A1.4)

Example Graph (Figure A1.5)

Graph (blank, Figure A1.6)

Blackline A1.1

Measurement and Statistics

Task Explanation and Suggested Procedures

Task:	Determine who has the biggest pumpkin.

Suggested Procedures:

1. Discuss the methods you could use to determine who has the biggest pumpkin.
2. Choose at least one method.
3. Collect and record group data.
4. Make a bar graph of the data. Make sure you include all of the needed information.
5. Complete reflections page independently.

Names of Group Members	_____ (Data being collected)

Figure A1.2

SkyLight Professional Development

Measurement and Statistics

Reflections

Describe the method your group chose to determine who had the biggest pumpkin. Explain why that method was chosen.

_____

_____

_____

_____

_____

_____

_____

_____

_____

What did you learn today?

_____

_____

Was there something that you liked about math class today?

_____

_____

Was there something that you would have liked to do differently?

_____

_____

Figure A1.3

Measurement and Statistics

Rubric

	0	1	2	3
Graph Title	No title	Title does not relate to the graph.	Title relates to graph. Capitalization or spelling error present.	Title relates to graph. Capitalization and spelling are perfect.
Axes Labeled	No labels	Labels do not relate to graph.	Labels relate to graph. Capitalization or spelling error present.	Labels relate to graph. Capitalization and spelling are perfect.
x-axis information	Not present	Information present but inappropriate.	Information present with errors.	Information present and accurate.
y-axis information	Not present	Axis numbered incorrectly.	Axis numbered correctly.	Axis numbered correctly and neatly.
Graph accuracy	Incomplete	Graph complete but inaccurate.	Graph complete. and accurate.	Graph complete, accurate and neat.

Evaluator: _____   Points possible = 15   Points earned = _____

Figure A1.4

Measurement and Statistics

Example Graph

Not sure what goes where? Use this as a model.

The Great Pumpkin

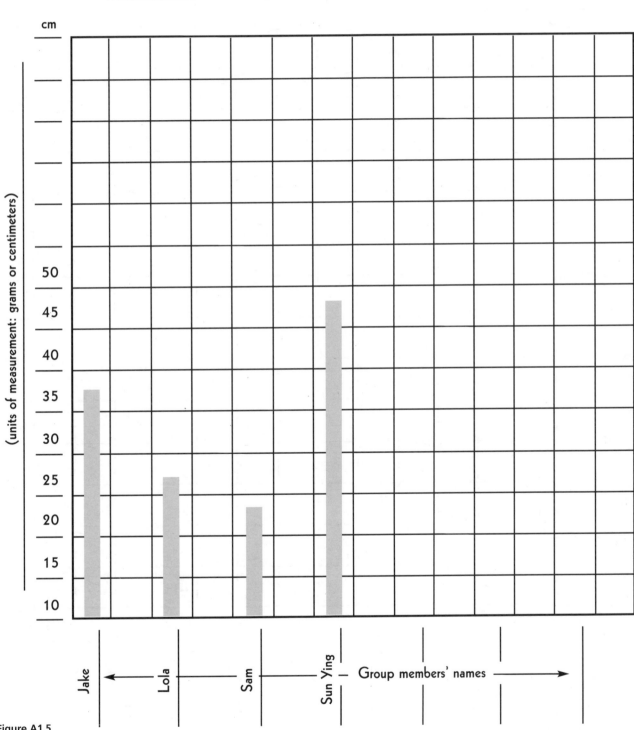

Figure A1.5

Measurement and Statistics

Graph

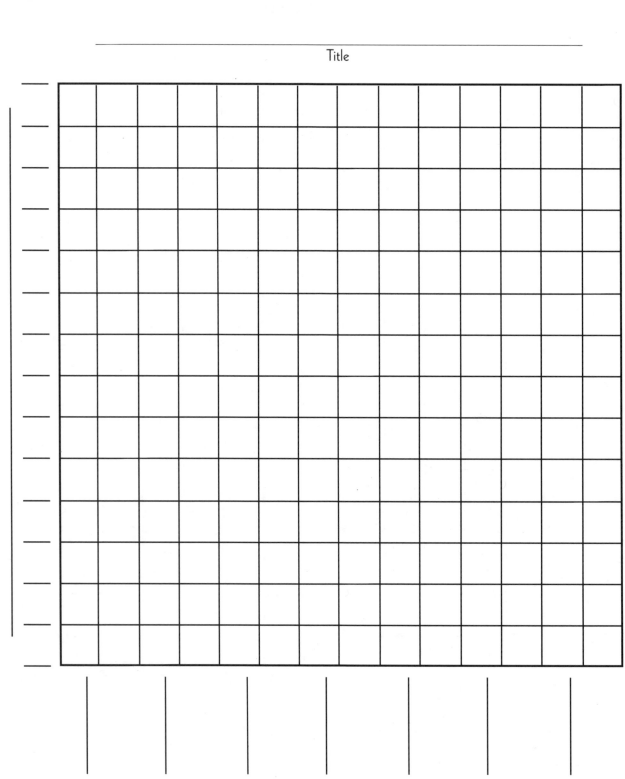

_____

Title

▪ PROJECT 2 OVERVIEW ▪
Symmetry and Area

STANDARDS Geometry, Communication, Problem Solving

MATHEMATICS CONCEPTS Symmetry and area

GRADE LEVELS 4 through 10

MATERIALS NEEDED Graph paper, standard rulers

TASK The Atlas Tile Company is looking for new 8" by 8" floor tile patterns. Company requirements say that all tiles must have at least one line of symmetry and be made of a variety of polygons with various sizes and shapes. Polygons should be covered with patterns to add interest to the floor tile. When the tile is complete, the people at Atlas need to know the exact area of each pattern in the tile. This will help with ordering materials. They also need an explanation as to how much material will be needed to cover a 12' by 18' floor.

SUGGESTED STUDENT PROCEDURES

1. Using an 8" by 8" piece of graph paper and a ruler, draw a mosaic tile. The tile should be made up of various polygons of different sizes and shapes and have at least one line of symmetry.

2. Shapes within the tile should be decorated with at least six different colors or patterns.

3. Determine the amount of each pattern or color needed to recreate the tile. (Find area in square inches)

4. Draw the tile and an organizational chart showing the patterns, formulas, and the amount of material needed to complete each pattern within the tile.

5. Write an explanation telling the amount of each pattern needed to complete a 12' by 18' floor.

TEACHER RESOURCES

Sample Tile and Organizational Chart (Figure A1.8)

Sample Solution (Figure A1.9)

Rubrics (Figures A1.10 and A1.11)

Blackline A1.7

Symmetry and Area
Sample Tile and Organizational Chart

Pattern	Amount and Shape	Formula and Area	Total Area
	4 triangles	$\frac{1}{2}(3 \times 1) = 1.5$	6 inches^2
	4 triangles	$\frac{1}{2}(3 \times 2) = 3$	12 inches^2
	4 triangles	$\frac{1}{2}(1.5 \times 2) = 1.5$	6 inches^2
	1 square	$2 \times 2 = 4$	4 inches^2
	2 triangles	$\frac{1}{2}(3 \times 4) = 6$	12 inches^2
	4 triangles	$\frac{1}{2}(1 \times 1) = .5$	2 inches^2
	4 triangles	$\frac{1}{2}(1 \times 1) = .5$	2 inches^2
	8 triangles	$\frac{1}{2}(1 \times 1) = .5$	4 inches^2
	2 triangles	$\frac{1}{2}(3 \times 4) = 6$	12 inches^2
	2 triangles	$\frac{1}{2}(2 \times 1) = 1$	2 inches^2
	2 triangles	$\frac{1}{2}(2 \times 1) = 1$	2 inches^2

Total = 64 inches^2

Figure A1.8

SkyLight Professional Development

Symmetry and Area

Sample Solution

How many square inches of each pattern are needed to cover a 12' x 18' floor?
(One square equals one square foot.)

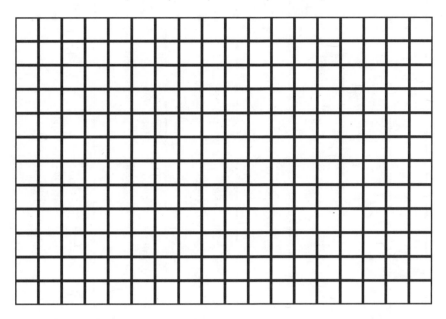

On a 12' x 18' floor, three tiles are needed for every two feet of space. For that reason 27 tiles are needed along the base and 18 are needed for the height. A total of 18' x 27', or 486 tiles are necessary to cover the floor. To determine how much of each pattern is needed, the total square inches can be multiplied by 486.

Teacher Notes

Students who are comfortable with performance tasks will not need to be given suggested procedures.

Sample answers are suggestions. Students will vary depending on their tile.

Rubrics should be distributed before beginning the task.

Computers could also be used to complete the project.

Figure A1.9

Symmetry and Area

Symmetry and Area Rubric

Highlight the descriptor for each criteria that best fits the product. Add points earned to determine total rubric score.

	1	2	3	4
Tile Shapes and sizes	4 or less different shapes or sizes used	5–6 different shapes or sizes used	7–8 different shapes or sizes used	9 or more different shapes or sizes used
Patterns	4 or less different patterns used	5–6 different patterns used	7–8 different patterns used	9 or more different patterns used
Line of Symmetry	Tile is not symmetrical	Not applicable	Not applicable	Tile has 1 or more lines of symmetry
Neatness	Sloppy; ruler or computer not used	Ruler or computer used, shapes overlap or have space in between	Ruler or computer used, shapes neatly aligned	Ruler or computer used, shapes neatly aligned, tile looks professional
Organizational Chart	Disorganized; doesn't contain formulas/equations, area, or patterns	Organized; some information missing (formulas/equations, area, or patterns)	Organized; patterns, formulas/equations, and area information is present	Organized and neat; formulas/equations, patterns, and area information are present
Formulas/Equations	3 or more missing or incorrect	All present, 1–2 incorrect	All present and correct and written accurately	All present, correct, written accurately and neatly
Areas	3 or more missing or incorrect	All present, 1–2 incorrect	All present and correct	All present and correct including inches^2
Total Areas	3 or more missing or incorrect	All present, 1–2 incorrect	All present and correct	All present and correct including inches^2

Student name: _____   Evaluator: _____   Points possible = 32   Points earned = _____

Figure A1.10

Symmetry and Area

Symmetry and Area Explanation Rubric

Highlight the descriptor for each criteria that best fits the product. Add points earned to determine total rubric score.

	1	2	3	4
Explanation Spelling and Grammar	4 or more spelling or grammar errors	2–3 spelling or grammar errors	1 spelling or grammar error	Spelling and grammar perfect!
Clarity	Difficult to understand	Unclear in parts	Clearly written	Clearly written, well explained
Neatness	Sloppy	Can be read with careful concentration	Neatly written	Neatly typed

Student Name: _____ Evaluator: _____ Points Possible = 12   Points earned = ____

▪ PROJECT 3 OVERVIEW ▪
Standard Measurement

STANDARDS   Measurement, Communication, Problem Solving

MATHEMATICS CONCEPTS   Standard measurement of length and weight, area

GRADE LEVELS   4 through 8

MATERIALS NEEDED   Standard rulers and scale, graph paper, assorted stuffed bean bag animals

TASK   The Teenie Stuffed Critter Company needs to make more Teenie Stuffed Critters for giveaways for The Better Burger Corporation. To order materials, they need to know how much fabric and filler is needed to make the various critters.

SUGGESTED STUDENT PROCEDURES

1. Each individual or cooperative group will receive bean bag animals.

2. Weigh each bean bag animal to the smallest unit possible with the scale provided.

3. Using $\frac{1}{4}$ inch graph paper and a ruler, draw a two-dimensional diagram of the bean bag animal and its parts. The diagram should include all pieces of fabric necessary to construct the toy and may be drawn in parts. The colors needed should be labeled for each part drawn.

4. Include all measurements to the nearest $\frac{1}{4}$ inch. Make as many measurements as necessary to accurately label all parts of the creature.

5. Use the measurements and the drawing to find the approximate amount of fabric needed for each part of the bean bag animal.

6. Create a chart including bean bag animal name, weight, colors, and amount of fabric needed. Attach it to the drawing.

7. Write a summary of your findings.

TEACHER RESOURCES

Sample Page (Figure A1.13)

Rubric (Figure A1.14)

Figure A1.12

Standard Measurement

Sample Page

Teenie Stuffed Critter: Nuts the Squirrel   Weight = _____ ounces

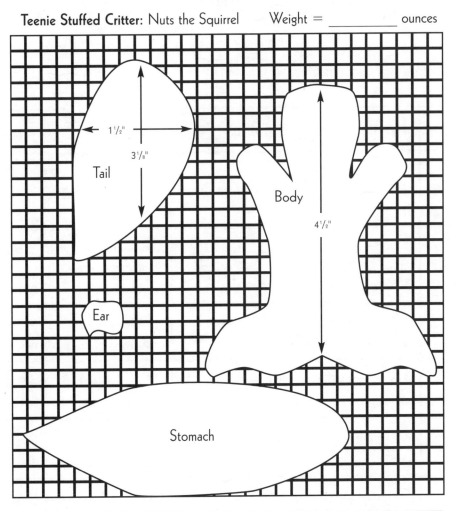

Body Part	Color	Approximate Area
Tail	Brown fur	_____ inches²
Ear	2 brown 2 white	_____ inches²
Body	Brown	_____ inches²
Stomach	White	_____ inches²

Figure A.13

Standard Measurement

Rubric

Highlight the descriptor for each criteria that best fits the product. Add points earned to determine total rubric score.

	1 point	2 points	3 points	4 points
Body Parts Drawing	1 or more parts missing	Parts present, drawn inaccurately	Parts drawn accurately	Parts drawn accurately and neatly
Labeling	1 or more labels missing	Labels present, 1 or more spelled inaccurately	Labels present, spelled accurately	Labels present, spelled accurately, neat
Measurements	3 or more missing or inaccurate	1–2 missing or inaccurate	All present and accurate	All present, accurate, and neat
Area	1 or more missing or inaccurate	Not applicable	All present and accurate	All present, accurate and neat
Weight	Missing or inaccurate	Not applicable	Present and accurate	Present, accurate, and neat
Chart	1 or more categories missing	All categories present	Present and accurate	Present, accurate, and constructed with ruler or computer
Explanation	Missing or confusing	Ideas could be stated more clearly	Clearly stated	Clearly stated and easy to understand

Student name: _____   Evaluator: _____

Points possible = 28   Points earned = _____

Figure A1.14

■ PROJECT 4 OVERVIEW ■
Unit Pricing

STANDARDS   Decimal Operations, Communication, Problem Solving

MATHEMATICS CONCEPTS   Unit pricing

GRADE LEVELS   4 through 9

MATERIALS NEEDED   Grocery items

TASK   Mrs. Jones just moved into your neighborhood and wants your input with her grocery shopping. She is trying to decide which product size is generally the best buy. She wants your help.

SUGGESTED STUDENT PROCEDURES

1. Choose the largest and smallest size of any ten items in a grocery store. (Note: If it is not possible for you to go to the grocery store, your teacher will bring two sizes of ten items into the classroom.)

2. Record the name of each item, the size or quanity of each item, and the price of each item.
   Example: Hot Dogs   12 ounces $0.78
                                    16 ounces $1.04

3. Determine the unit price of each item and indicate which size is the better buy. (To find the unit price, divide the price by the number of ounces and round to the nearest cent.)

4. Complete the reflections page.

TEACHER RESOURCES

Data Collection Chart (Figure A.16)

Rubric (Figure A.17)

Reflections Page (Figure A.18)

Figure A1.15

Unit Pricing

Data Collection Chart

Item Name	Size #1	Price #1	Unit Price #1	Size #2	Price #2	Unit Price #2	Better Buy
1.							
2.							
3.							
4.							
5.							
6.							
7.							
8.							
9.							
10.							

Figure A1.16

Unit Pricing

Rubric

Highlight each square that best describes the performance.

	0	1	2	3
Unit Pricing Item 1	Both missing or inaccurate	1 missing or inaccurate	Both accurate	Both accurate and rounded to the nearest cent
Item 2	Both missing or inaccurate	1 missing or inaccurate	Both accurate	Both accurate and rounded to the nearest cent
Item 3	Both missing or inaccurate	1 missing or inaccurate	Both accurate	Both accurate and rounded to the nearest cent
Item 4	Both missing or inaccurate	1 missing or inaccurate	Both accurate	Both accurate and rounded to the nearest cent
Item 5	Both missing or inaccurate	1 missing or inaccurate	Both accurate	Both accurate and rounded to the nearest cent
Item 6	Both missing or inaccurate	1 missing or inaccurate	Both accurate	Both accurate and rounded to the nearest cent
Item 7	Both missing or inaccurate	1 missing or inaccurate	Both accurate	Both accurate and rounded to the nearest cent
Item 8	Both missing or inaccurate	1 missing or inaccurate	Both accurate	Both accurate and rounded to the nearest cent
Item 9	Both missing or inaccurate	1 missing or inaccurate	Both accurate	Both accurate and rounded to the nearest cent
Item 10	Both missing or inaccurate	1 missing or inaccurate	Both accurate	Both accurate and rounded to the nearest cent
Better Buys	3 or more errors	2 errors	1 error	All accurate
Spelling	3 or more errors	2 errors	1 error	All accurate
Neatness	Difficult to read	Can be read with careful concentration	Neat	Perfect letters and numbers
Reflections	Difficult to understand	Lack clarity	Easy to understand	Easy to understand, show deep understanding of unit pricing

Student name: _____   Evaluator: _____   Points possible = 56   Points earned: _____

Figure A.17

Unit Pricing

Reflections

Name_____

After compiling your data, what conclusions can you draw? Support your statements with examples.

Reflections:

Figure A.18

■ PROJECT 5 OVERVIEW ■

Complementary and Supplementary Angles

STANDARDS   Geometry, Communication, Problem Solving

MATHEMATICS CONCEPTS   Understanding and creating complementary and supplementary angles

GRADE LEVELS   6 through 10

MATERIALS NEEDED   Examples of complementary and supplementary angles, protractors, scissors, glue, assorted colored paper

PURPOSE

1. To give students experience measuring angles using a protractor.

2. To give students experience finding and creating complementary and supplementary angles.

SUGGESTED STUDENT PROCEDURES

1. On the paper provided, explain the meaning of complementary and supplementary angles.

2. Determine four pairs each of complementary and supplementary angles.
   Example: $42° + 48° = 90°$
                  $115° + 65° = 180°$

3. Using a protractor and a separate piece of colored paper, draw each angle and label it with the appropriate number of degrees. Cut out each angle. Keep each angle with its pair.
   Example:

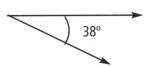
38°

4. Fit the angle pairs onto the Supplementary Angles or Complementary Angles work page provided to show that they actually are complementary or supplementary angles. The fit should be exact. If it is not, make sure the angle size is correct and that it was cut carefully.
   Example:

TEACHER RESOURCES

Complementary and Supplementary Angle Work Pages (Figures A1.20 and A1.21)

Rubric (Figure A1.22)

Figure A1.19

Complementary and Supplementary Angles

Supplementary Angles

Description: _____

_____

_____

_____ + _____ = 180°

_____ + _____ = 180°

Figure A1.20

Complementary and Supplementary Angles

Complementary Angles

Description: _____

_____

_____

_____ + _____ = 90°

_____ + _____ = 90°

Figure A1.21

Complementary and Supplementary Angles

Complementary and Supplementary Angles Rubric

Circle the point value of the description that best applies to the finished product.

Complementary Angles Description	Description accurate and understandable. Example of concept included with definition. Spelling is perfect. Words are neatly written.	4
	Description accurate and understandable. Spelling is perfect. Words are neatly written.	3
	Description may be accurate but is difficult to understand OR spelling may be inaccurate OR neatness needs improvement.	2
	Description is difficult to understand, some spelling inaccuracies.	1
Pairs of Angles	Four angle pairs, neatly and accurately labeled each with sums of 90°	4
	Four angle pairs, accurately labeled each with sums of 90°	3
	Four angle pairs, accurately labeled	2
	Four angle pairs	1
Angle Measurement and Placement	Four angle pairs, drawn accurately and neatly glued to work pages showing that they are complementary	4
	Four angle pairs, drawn accurately and glued to work pages showing that they are complemenary	3
	Four angle pairs, drawn accurately and glued to work pages	2
	Four angle pairs glued to work pages	1
Supplementary Angles Description	Description accurate and understandable. Example of concept included with definition. Spelling is perfect. Words are neatly written.	4
	Description accurate and understandable. Spelling is perfect. Words are neatly written.	3
	Description may be accurate but is difficult to understand OR spelling may be inaccurate OR neatness needs improvement.	2
	Description is difficult to understand, some spelling inaccuracies.	1
Pairs of Angles	Four angles pairs, neatly and accurately labeled each with sums of 180°	4
	Four angle pairs, accurately labeled each with sums of 180°	3
	Four angle pairs, accurately labeled	2
	Four angle pairs	1
Angle Measurement and Placement	Four angle pairs, drawn accurately and neatly glued to work pages showing that they are supplementary.	4
	Four angle pairs, drawn accurately and glued to work pages showing that they are supplementary.	3
	Four angle pairs, drawn accurately and glued to work pages.	2
	Four angle pairs glued to work pages.	1

Student name: _____   Evaluator: _____   Points possible = 24 Points earned = _____

Figure A1.22

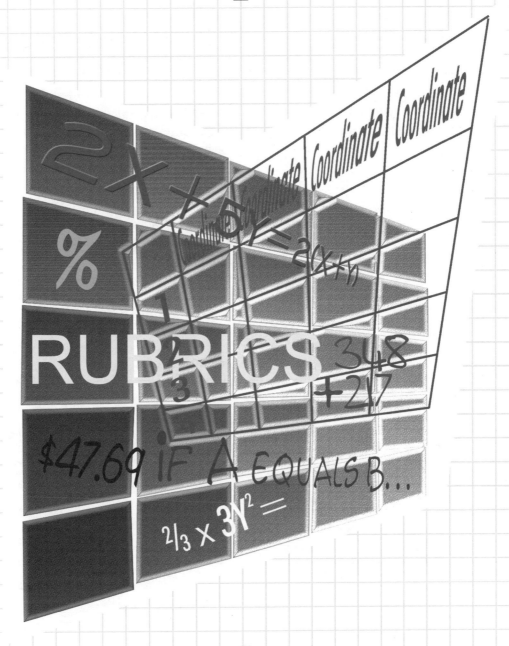

Turning a 4-Point Rubric Score into a Letter Grade

Turning a 4-Point Rubric Score into a Letter Grade

When using a four-point rubric, like the one below, a score of three shows students are achieving at an acceptable level. After all, it is the second highest point value on the rubric. However, teachers who need to use letter grades are in a bind when grading this way. Often the easiest way to grade is to take the score earned on the rubric and turn it into a percent. Mathematically this is accomplished by dividing the points earned by the number of points possible. But, this method alone will not give an accurate picture of student achievement. When earning three points on a four-point rubric, a student has performed well. Three out of four points mathematically, however, is only a score of 75%. In many grading systems, the student is now left with an undeserved "D."

Out of fairness to the students, and to calculate a more accurate reflection of student performance, the numbers can be manipulated slightly to achieve a grade that is more indicative of the quality of the product.

Name_____   Date_____

Solving Equations Grading Rubric

Criteria	1	2	3	4
Equation solution	Answer only is shown	Initial equation and answer only are shown	Initial equation, steps and answers are shown	Initial equation, all steps and answer are shown
Equation answer	Answer is incorrect	Steps are incorrect or not present, but answer is correct	Steps are correct, but answer is incorrect	Steps are correct and answer is correct
Explanation of solution	Explanation is present, but demonstrates a lack of understanding	Explanation indicates a minimal understanding of procedure	Explanation indicates procedures are understood	Explanation clearly indicates procedures are understood at an advanced level

Points possible = 12   Points earned = 10

Figure A2.1

In the rubric shown above (Figure A2.1), this student would receive an 83% as a result of her rubric score if the evaluator changes it into a percent. If that is the desired method, the evaluator could try using one of the options shown in Figures A2.2 and A2.3 and A2.4 to determine the letter grade. These options might provide a fairer picture of achievement.

Option One

Turn the rubric score into a percent by dividing the points earned by the points possible, then use the scale provided.

Example:

Student earns 10 out of 12 points. $10 \div 12 = 83\%$ $83\% = B$

88–100	=	A
75–87	=	B
62–74	=	C
50–61	=	D
0–50	=	F

This is a suggested point scale that seems to work fairly well. Percents can be adjusted up or down to best meet the needs of students.

Figure A2.2

Figure A2.3 shows another option that can be used when assigning a grade to a point value.

Option Two

Determine the total points possible for the rubric. Divide the total possible by 5 to determine the increments for each point group. This is done because there are 5 grades in the A, B, C, D, F grading scale.

Example: rubric points possible total = 12 $12/5 = 2.4$

The (quotient) answer determines the highest point value for the "F" group.

  F = 0–2.4 points

To determine the highest value for the "D" group, add the quotient to the highest point value in the "F" group.

  D = 2.41–4.8 points

To determine the highest value for the "C" group, add the quotient to the highest point value in the "D" group.

  C = 4.81–7.2 points

To determine the highest value for the "B" group, add the quotient to the highest point value in the "C" group.

  B = 7.21–9.6 points

To determine the highest value for the "A" group add the quotient to the highest point value in the "B" group.

  A = 9.61–12 points

Figure A2.3

Option Three:

Determine the points earned and divide by the number of criteria scored in the rubric. The answer will be a number between 1 and 4 when the rubric has a 1-4 point scale.

Example: On a 4-point rubric with 3 criteria, a student scores 10 points.

$10 \div 3 = 3.33$ $3.33 = B$

1–4 Rubric scale	**1–4 Rubric scale**	**0–3 Rubric scale**
no zero used	with optional use of	
	zero for no evidence	
A = 3.41–4.0	of a performance	A = 2.41–3.0
B = 2.81–3.4	A = 3.21–4.0	B = 1.81–2.4
C = 2.21–2.8	B = 2.41–3.2	C = 1.21–1.8
D = 1.61–2.2	C = 1.61–2.4	D = 0.61–1.2
F = 1.0–1.6	D = 0.81–1.6	F = 0.0–0.6
	F = 0.0–0.8	

Figure A2.4

A third option is demonstrated in Figure A2.4.

Each of these options aims to change a four-point rubric scale into a five-point letter grade scale. Using any of the three options provided should give teachers a more realistic picture of student achievement.

Bibliography

Ainsworth, L. and J. Christinson. 1998. *Student generated rubrics.* Orangeburg, NY: Dale Seymour Publications.

Allen, P. 1996, May. *Educational issues series: performance assessment.* Wisconsin Education Association Council.

Battista, M. 1999. The mathematical miseducation of America's youth. *Phi Delta Kappan,* February, 425–33.

Bay, J., B. Reys, and R. Reys. 1999. The top 10 elements that must be in place to implement standards-based mathematics curricula. *Phi Delta Kappan,* March, 503–506.

Black, P. and D. Wiliam. 1998. *Inside the black box: Raising standards through classroom assessment. Phi Delta Kappan Online.* http://www.pdkintl.org/kappan/kbla9810.htm (Accessed January 2001).

Black, S. 1994. Doing the numbers. *The Executive Educator,* March, 41–44.

Bryant, D. and M. Driscoll. 1998. *Exploring classroom assessment in mathematics.* Reston, VA: National Council of Teachers of Mathematics.

Buehl, D. 1995. *Classroom strategies for interactive learning.* Schofield, WI: Wisconsin State Reading Association (WSRA) Publications.

Burke, K. 1999. *How to assess authentic learning.* Arlington Heights, IL: Skylight Training and Publishing.

Caudell, L. 1996, Fall. *High stakes. NW Education Magazine Online.* http://www.nrel.org/nwedu/fall_96/article6.html (Accessed October 1998).

Childs, R. 1989. *Constructing classroom achievement tests.* ERIC Document, ED 315426.

Costa, A. and B. Kallick. 1995. *Assessment in the learning organization.* Alexandria, VA: Association for Supervision and Curriculum Development.

Crosswhite, J., et al. 1989. NCTM standards for school mathematics; visions for implementation. *Arithmetic Teacher,* May, 55–60.

Danielson, C. 1997. *A collection of performance tasks and rubrics.* Larchmont, NY: Eye On Education.

Dietel, R., J. Herman, and R. Knuth. 1991. *What does research say about assessment?* Oakbrook: North Central Regional Educational Laboratory (NCREL)

Eisner, E. *The uses and limits of performance assessment. Phi Delta Kappan Online.* http://www.pdkintl.org/kappan/keis9905.htm (Accessed January 2001).

Fitzpatrick, K. 1998. *Program evaluation: Mathematics.* Schaumburg, IL: National Study of School Evaluation (NSSE).

Frye, S. 1989. The NCTM standards, challenges for all classrooms. *Arithmetic Teacher,* 36:4–7.

Gardner, H. 1983. *Frames of mind: Theory of multiple intelligences.* New York: Basic Books.

Geocaris, C. and M. Ross. 1999. A test worth taking. *Educational Leadership,* September, 29–33.

Glaser, R. 1998. Reinventing assessment and accountability to help all children learn: Introductory remarks. National Center for Research on Evaluation, Standards, and Student Testing (CRESST) Conference.

Hatfield, M. and J. Price. 1992. Promoting local change: Models for implementing NCTM's curriculum and evaluation standards. *Arithmetic Teacher,* January, 34–37.

Jenkins, L. 1997. *Improving student learning.* Milwaukee, WI: ASQ Quality Press.

Kaplan, A. 1998. *Math on call.* Wilmington, MA: Great Source Education Group.

Kulm, G. 1999. Making sure that your mathematics curriculum meets standards. *Mathematics Teaching in Middle School,* 4(8): 536–541.

LaCoste, P. 1995. *Students grading students: Sharing responsibility for assessment.* Milwaukee, WI: University of Wisconsin–Milwaukee.

Lazear, D. 1994. *Seven pathways of learning.* Tucson, AZ: Zephyr Press.

Mabry, L. *Writing to the rubric: Lingering effects of traditional standardized testing on direct writing instruction. Phi Delta Kappan Online.* http:pdkintl.org/kappan/kmab9905.htm (Accessed May 1999).

Martin, H. 1996. *Integrating mathematics across the curriculum.* Arlington Heights, IL: IRI/Skylight Training and Publishing, Inc.

Marzano, R. and J. Kendall. 1996. *Designing standards-based districts, schools and classrooms.* Alexandria, VA: Association for Supervision and Curriculum Development.

McTighe, J. and G. Wiggins. 1999. *The understanding by design handbook.* Alexandria, VA: Association for Supervision and Curriculum Development.

Merriam-Webster. 1989. *The new Merriam-Webster dictionary.* Springfield, MA: Merriam-Webster.

Mullins, I., et al. 1993. *NAEP 1992 mathematics report card for the nation and the states.* Washington, DC: United States Department of Education, Office of Educational Research and Improvement.

Munk, D. and W. Bursick. 1997/1998. Can grades be helpful and fair? *Educational Leadership,* Dec/Jan, 44–47.

National Assessment of Educational Progress (NAEP). 1998. Mathematics Report Card for the Nation and the States. The Nation's Report Card. http://nces.ed.gov/nationsreportcard/96report/97488.html

National Council of Teachers of Mathematics (NCTM). 2000. *Principles and standards for school mathematics.* Reston, VA: National Council of Teachers of Mathematics.

O'Brien, T. 1999. Parrot math. *Phi Delta Kappan,* February, 434–38.

Reeves, D. 1998. *Making standards work.* Denver, CO: Center for Performance Assessment.

Rogers, S. and S. Graham. 1997. *The high performance toolbox.* Evergreen, CO: Peak Learning Systems.

Ronis, D. 1999. *Brain compatible mathematics.* Arlington Heights, IL: Skylight Training and Publishing, Inc.

Rose, M. 1999. Make room for rubrics. *Instructor,* March, 30–31.

Schmoker, M. 1996. *Results.* Alexandria, VA: Association for Supervision and Curriculum Development.

Schurr, S., J. Thomason, and M. Thomason. 1996. *Teaching at the middle.* Toronto, Ontario: D.C. Heath and Company.

Slavin, S. 1989. *All the math you'll ever need.* New York: Riley & Sons Inc.

Stiggins, R. 1995. *Sound performance assessments in the guidance context.* ERIC Document, ED388889.

United States Department of Education. 1993, April. *Help your child improve in test-taking.* US Department of Education Office of Research and Improvement.

United States Department of Education. 1996, Spring. *Improving America's schools: A newsletter on issues in school reform.* US Department of Education.

Wiggins, G. 1992, May. *Creating tests worth taking. Educational Leadership Online.* http://www.bbpages.psu.edu/bbpages_references/40001/400015437.html (Accessed October 1998).

Wolfe, P. and R. Brandt. 1998. What do we know from brain research? *Educational Leadership,* November, 8–13.

Zemelman, S., H. Daniels, and A. Hyde. 1993. *Best practices.* Portsmouth, NH: Heinemann.

Index

Index

SkyLight

PROFESSIONAL DEVELOPMENT

We Prepare Your Teachers Today for the Classrooms of Tomorrow

Learn from Our Books and from Our Authors!

Ignite Learning in Your School or District.

SkyLight's team of classroom-experienced consultants can help you foster systemic change for increased student achievement.

Professional development is a process not an event. SkyLight's experienced practitioners drive the creation of our on-site professional development programs, graduate courses, research-based publications, interactive video courses, teacher-friendly training materials, and online resources—call SkyLight Professional Development today.

SkyLight specializes in three professional development areas.

Specialty #

Best Practices

We **model** the best practices that result in improved student performance and guided applications.

Specialty #

Making the Innovations Last

We help set up **support** systems that make innovations part of everyday practice in the long-term systemic improvement of your school or district.

Specialty #

How to Assess the Results

We prepare your school leaders to encourage and **assess** teacher growth, **measure** student achievement, and **evaluate** program success.

Contact the SkyLight team and begin a process toward long-term results.

2626 S. Clearbrook Dr., Arlington Heights, IL 60005
800-348-4474 • 847-290-6600 • FAX 847-290-6609
info@skylightedu.com • www.skylightedu.com